AF782209

COMPUTER SCIENCE, TECHNOLOGY AND APPLICATIONS

NETWORK CODING AND DATA COMPRESSION

THEORY, APPLICATIONS AND CHALLENGES

Computer Science, Technology and Applications

Additional books in this series can be found on Nova's website under the Series tab.

Additional E-books in this series can be found on Nova's website under the E-book tab.

COMPUTER SCIENCE, TECHNOLOGY AND APPLICATIONS

NETWORK CODING AND DATA COMPRESSION

THEORY, APPLICATIONS AND CHALLENGES

MARYANN SIMMONS
EDITOR

nova publishers
New York

Copyright © 2015 by Nova Science Publishers, Inc.

All rights reserved. No part of this book may be reproduced, stored in a retrieval system or transmitted in any form or by any means: electronic, electrostatic, magnetic, tape, mechanical photocopying, recording or otherwise without the written permission of the Publisher.

We have partnered with Copyright Clearance Center to make it easy for you to obtain permissions to reuse content from this publication. Simply navigate to this publication's page on Nova's website and locate the "Get Permission" button below the title description. This button is linked directly to the title's permission page on copyright.com. Alternatively, you can visit copyright.com and search by title, ISBN, or ISSN.

For further questions about using the service on copyright.com, please contact:
Copyright Clearance Center
Phone: +1-(978) 750-8400 Fax: +1-(978) 750-4470 E-mail: info@copyright.com.

NOTICE TO THE READER

The Publisher has taken reasonable care in the preparation of this book, but makes no expressed or implied warranty of any kind and assumes no responsibility for any errors or omissions. No liability is assumed for incidental or consequential damages in connection with or arising out of information contained in this book. The Publisher shall not be liable for any special, consequential, or exemplary damages resulting, in whole or in part, from the readers' use of, or reliance upon, this material. Any parts of this book based on government reports are so indicated and copyright is claimed for those parts to the extent applicable to compilations of such works.

Independent verification should be sought for any data, advice or recommendations contained in this book. In addition, no responsibility is assumed by the publisher for any injury and/or damage to persons or property arising from any methods, products, instructions, ideas or otherwise contained in this publication.

This publication is designed to provide accurate and authoritative information with regard to the subject matter covered herein. It is sold with the clear understanding that the Publisher is not engaged in rendering legal or any other professional services. If legal or any other expert assistance is required, the services of a competent person should be sought. FROM A DECLARATION OF PARTICIPANTS JOINTLY ADOPTED BY A COMMITTEE OF THE AMERICAN BAR ASSOCIATION AND A COMMITTEE OF PUBLISHERS.

Additional color graphics may be available in the e-book version of this book.

Library of Congress Cataloging-in-Publication Data

Network coding and data compression : theory, applications and challenges / editors, Maryann Simmons.
pages cm. -- (Computer science, technology and applications)
Includes index.
ISBN 978-1-63483-185-7 (hardcover)
1. Coding theory. 2. Data compression (Computer science) 3. Computer networks. I. Simmons, Maryann.
TK5102.92.N475 2014
621.382'12--dc23

2015021921

Published by Nova Science Publishers, Inc. †New York

CONTENTS

PREFACE

In this book, new developments in network coding and data compression are examined. The first chapter proposes a new multipath transmission scheme that employs network coding at the source for rate-delay adaptation. The second chapter presents the theory, applications and challenges of a physical-layer network coding technique that promises significant improvement to the spectral efficiency and interference mitigation challenges in future heterogenous cellular and wireless networks. In this third chapter, network and distributed turbo coding based HARQ protocol are examined for wireless broadcasting systems. The last three chapters included in this book present three models that are based on Data Envelopment Analysis (DEA) methodology to appropriately evaluate the efficiency of multicast energy and further minimizes energy transmission in wireless networks without affecting the overall network performance; the development of methods of experimental statistical modeling of physical laws and the cascade scheme of data compression in multimode fiber systems.

In Chapter 1, the authors propose a new multipath transmission scheme that employs network coding at the source for rate-delay adaptation. The proposed scheme utilizes path diversity for transmitting network coded packets on different paths to enhance the information rate while providing statistical delay guarantees. They analyze the rate-delay tradeoffs of the proposed scheme and compare its performance with the repetition based multipath transmission scheme. The results show that multipath transmission efficiency can be improved via the proposed scheme.

The concept of network coding has emerged as a very promising technique that can be used to improve the efficiency of spectral utilization and systems throughput in wireless communications. In network coding, intermediate nodes or relays mix the information signals they receive and forward the mixture to several destinations simultaneously. Physical-layer Network Coding (PNC) defines a form of network coding which could convert interfering signals to an harmless phenomenon directly from modulated and demodulated signals at the physical-layer. PNC equally provides a means to eliminate the interference-induced scrambling of signals which results in packet collisions at the medium access control layer of existing wireless networks. Chapter 2 presents the theory, applications and challenges of a physical-layer network coding technique that promises significant improvement to the spectral efficiency and interference mitigation challenges in future heterogeneous cellular and wireless networks. Specifically, examples of PNC application in Femtocell-Macrocell overlay network are presented.

A major challenge with wireless and cellular systems is maintaining a balance between reliable communication and higher spatial reuse of the spectrum. One promising resolution technique is by using femtocells to bring the receiver nearer to the transmitter. A Femtocell-Macrocell overlay network forms an heterogeneous network which significantly improves the indoor coverage and provides better mobile user experience. Interference is generally undesirable in such an heterogeneous network because it causes collisions, corrupts received signals, and wastes limited bandwidth. For instance, in a macrocell-femtocell overlay network, radio frequency interference will result from a macrocell interfering with a femtocell or vice versa and such interference may considerably degrade the performance of the cellular system. Instead of viewing interference as a counterproductive phenomenon that should be avoided, this chapter provides a PNC scheme that transforms interference into a safe and beneficial phenomenon. This is due to the ability of PNC to embrace electromagnetic interference, improve spectral efficiency and achieve throughput optimality, thus making PNC suitable for the heterogeneous cellular network. The book chapter discussed different applications of a PNC scheme that exploits the interference of concurrent transmissions at the femtocell to increase network throughput and mitigate the interference.

Wireless broadcasting systems employ multiple retransmissions to guarantee the correct reception of each packet. Traditional hybrid automatic retransmission request (HARQ) protocol retransmits one packet per slot. Hence, a large amount of retransmissions is required to correctly receive all the packets, which leads to low spectrum efficiency. In Chapter 3, the authors propose a Network coding and distributed Turbo Coding based type-III HARQ (NTC-HARQ) protocol, including XORing Network Coding Combined

(XNCC) retransmission strategy at the access node (AN) and joint network-turbo decoding (JNTD) strategy at the user equipment (UE). Specifically, to reduce the overall number of retransmissions, lost packets of different UEs are network coding (NC) combined at the AN by utilizing XNCC strategy. The soft information of the lost packet at each UE can be recovered from the received network coded retransmission packet by using the proposed XORing soft network decoder. The recovered soft information of the UE's lost packet is combined with the local undecodable soft information of the same packet to form a distributed turbo code. A chase combining based distributed turbo decoder is proposed to perform turbo decoding, which introduces coding gain and improves Packet Error Rate (PER) performance. Theoretical analyses and simulation results show that the average number of transmissions performance of the proposed NTC-HARQ protocol outperforms that of the XNCC base type-I HARQ protocol (XNCC-HARQ), traditional NC based HARQ protocol (NC-HARQ) and JNTD based protocol (NC-JNTD).

In routing, the problem of performing minimum energy multicast considering Wireless Multicast Advantage (WMA) is difficult. This is because, the problem of minimum energy broadcast that is solved easily in the wire line case by various minimum weights panning tree algorithms, becomes NP-complete. However, alternative approach using heuristics method is employed. An example of this method is the Multicast Incremental Power (MIP) algorithm. The coding technique has further simplified the problem of minimum energy multicast. This is achieved by solving the problem of minimum energy multicast in polynomial time. As a result, optimal energy is less when coding is used compared to routing technique. Hence, coding in packet networks (network coding) is a promising approach for minimum energy multicast. Simulation results have shown that coding can reduce between 13% to 49% average total multicast energy in random wireless networks of varying size over MIP technique. Therefore, in terms of reducing the multicast energy, coded packet technique outperformed the MIP technique. Furthermore, it was observed that polynomial-time solution is not enough to address the problem of minimum energy multicast. This is because the solution was based on centralised computation, which is not suitable for many applications. As a result, a decentralized solution was proposed for optimisation in network coding. However, there is a need to further reduce the multicast energy in coded packet networks using appropriate model. This study reveals that though various solutions were proposed for minimum energy multicast but, they did not address the efficiency of the networks adequately. This rendered both the centralized and decentralised coding techniques inefficient. Chapter 4 seeks to answer the questions: How a network performance could be evaluated against the best-practice frontier networks? How could expected minimum energy in wireless network be achieved? These questions are addressed by studying the minimum energy multicast over coded packet networks and proposed alternative method based on empirical Data Envelopment Analysis (DEA) methodology. The study shows that substantial amount of energy could be reduced if the right model is used and the networks operate efficiently. The results are then analysed and compared with the current techniques.

A physical law can be most generally experimentally modeled by the probability distribution of measured variables. For this purpose the kernel estimator determined by experimental samples of variables is applicable. When experimental samples are overwhelming it is reasonable to use less numerous prototype samples. In this case a prototype represents experimental samples taking place in its surrounding. In our treatment the interval of the surrounding is described by the standard deviation of instrument output scattering at calibration. In Chapter 5, an algorithm is proposed for creation of prototypes and their adaptation to experimental samples that yields a proper model. This process is quantitatively characterized by changes of the cost function that is expressed by the information entropy. The number of created prototypes is generally much smaller than the number of experimental samples although the information provided by experimental data is well preserved. The compression procedure is demonstrated on analytically determined chaotic data and measured samples of traffic flow. Its performance is characterized by various information statistics.

Cooperative application of different data compression methods is an evident way to build advanced fiber systems with high information capacity. Intensive investigations resulted in development of the techniques that form the groups of time division multiplexing (TDM) and wavelength division multiplexing (WDM) methods. Furthermore, progress in fiber manufacturing technology enables fabricating multimode fibers demonstrating enhanced performances that allow using another data compression method – mode division multiplexing (MDM). Therefore, three-level hierarchic scheme of data compression in multimode fiber systems can be composed. The use of the techniques of TDM method is the content of the first stage. At the second stage, compressed information channels must be combined by WDM techniques. And the MDM technique should be applied at the highest hierarchic stage providing independent transmission of obtained complex information channels over the same multimode fiber. Combination of TDM and WDM techniques is realizable in practice, whereas application of MDM technique at the third stage depends on performances of the units providing selective mode excitation in multimode fibers. In chapter 6, results of experimental study of the developed selective waveguide element which could demonstrate perceptible spectral sensitivity show that this element is capable of providing cooperative application of WDM and MDM techniques. Hence, these results prove realizability of three-stage cascade scheme. Important advantageous feature of the cascade scheme is additional enhancement of data security in the system due to application of MDM technique.

In: Network Coding and Data Compression
Editor: M. Simmons
ISBN: 978-1-63483-185-7
© 2015 Nova Science Publishers, Inc.

Chapter 1

NETWORK CODING AT THE SOURCE: EXPLOITING MULTIPATH TRANSMISSION FOR RATE-DELAY ADAPTATION

Pin-Yu Chen*
Department of Electrical Engineering and Computer Science,
University of Michigan, Ann Arbor, MI, US

Abstract

In this chapter, we propose a new multipath transmission scheme that employs network coding at the source for rate-delay adaptation. The proposed scheme utilizes path diversity for transmitting network coded packets on different paths to enhance the information rate while providing statistical delay guarantees. We analyze the rate-delay trade-offs of the proposed scheme and compare its performance with the repetition based multipath transmission scheme. The results show that multipath transmission efficiency can be improved via the proposed scheme.

Keywords: Multipath transmission, network coding, rate-delay adaptation

*E-mail address: pinyu@umich.edu

1. Introduction

Multipath transmissions are proposed to meet the stringent quality-of-service (QoS) requirements by utilizing path diversity to reduce its latency, and they have been widely discussed in several communication paradigms, including wireless ad hoc networks, wired networks, and cognitive radio networks, to name a few. Typical examples are diverse routing in wired networks [1], coordinated multipoint transmissions in cellular systems [2], and multipath routing in cognitive radio networks [3]. In practice, disjoint paths can be found by periodically updating routing tables in wired networks, mesh networks and wireless networks with centralized infrastructure, while for wireless ad hoc networks, disjoint paths can be discovered via link reversal protocols [4].

In a nutshell, multipath transmission introduces redundancy on these paths (e.g., transmitting repeated packets) to trade for reduced latency. Therefore to fully utilize the advantage of multipath transmission one must adjust the redundancy to enhance the information rate while satisfying the required delay constraints. These aspects motivate this chapter to propose an efficient rate-delay adaptation scheme for multipath transmission [5, 6].

Traditionally, path diversity is exploited by erasure coding to protect communication between a source and destination pair connected by multiple disjoint paths [7, 8]. Native packets are encoded into many subpackets and the destination is able to decode the original data if it receives sufficient number of subpackets. Recently, in addition to achieving multicast network capacity, network coding [9, 10] is proposed to enhance the reliability by transmitting linearly encoded packetson disjoint paths [11, 12]. In [13], two source nodes exchange their information through the intermediate (relay) node via network coding to reduce the power consumption at the cost of additional delay.

Distinct from the above research mainly focusing on the rate-reliability (rate-diversity) tradeoffs [14] or energy-delay tradeoffs [13], we propose yet another application of network coding in multihop networks, where network coding is employed at the source for rate-delay adaptation. Compared with current repetition based scheme as the performance benchmark, where replicated data are transmitted through disjoint paths aiming to reduce the end-to-end delay, our proposed scheme provides better rate-delay tradeoffs with fine granularity, and it can be adjusted according to statistical delay constraint to enhance the performance of multipath transmissions.

2. System Model

Suppose there are D disjoint paths between the source and destination, and single path alone fails to support the end-to-end delay requirement of the delivered packet (otherwise the packet delivery is trivial). Let $\mathcal{P}_i$ denote the packet delivered through the ith path, which is a vector of length v over a Galois Field with size q, GF(q). For repetition based scheme, each packet is duplicated and sent through L disjoint paths. For network coding based scheme, N native packets are delivered through paths 1 to N, and M encoded packets are delivered through paths $N+1$ to $N+M$. We have

$$\mathcal{P}_i = \begin{cases} \mathcal{P}_i, & 1 \leq i \leq N, \\ \sum_{k=1}^{N} a_{i,k}\mathcal{P}_k, & N+1 \leq i \leq N+M, \end{cases} \tag{1}$$

where $a_{i,k} \in \text{GF}(q)$, $a_{i,k} \neq 0$ and each encoded packet is a linear combination of the N native packets. The encoding matrix $\mathcal{A}$ can be represented as

$$\mathcal{A} = \begin{bmatrix} 1 & 0 & \cdots & 0 \\ 0 & 1 & \cdots & 0 \\ \vdots & \vdots & \ddots & \vdots \\ 0 & 0 & \cdots & 1 \\ a_{N+1,1} & a_{N+1,2} & \cdots & a_{N+1,N} \\ a_{N+2,1} & a_{N+2,2} & \cdots & a_{N+2,N} \\ \vdots & \vdots & \ddots & \vdots \\ a_{N+M,1} & a_{N+M,2} & \cdots & a_{N+M,N} \end{bmatrix}_{(N+M)\times N}$$

$$\triangleq \begin{bmatrix} \mathcal{I}_{N\times N} \\ \mathcal{E}_{M\times N} \end{bmatrix}, \tag{2}$$

where $\mathcal{I}$ is an identity matrix, and the elements $a_{i,k}$ in $\mathcal{E}$ are chosen such that any N out of $N+M$ rows of matrix $\mathcal{A}$ are linearly independent. The encoding matrix $\mathcal{A}$ can be easily constructed when the field size q is large enough and each coefficient $a_{i,k}$ is randomly chosen from GF(q) [15]. Note that in this scheme we require $D \geq 3$, $N \geq 2$, $M \geq 1$ and $D - N - M \geq 0$

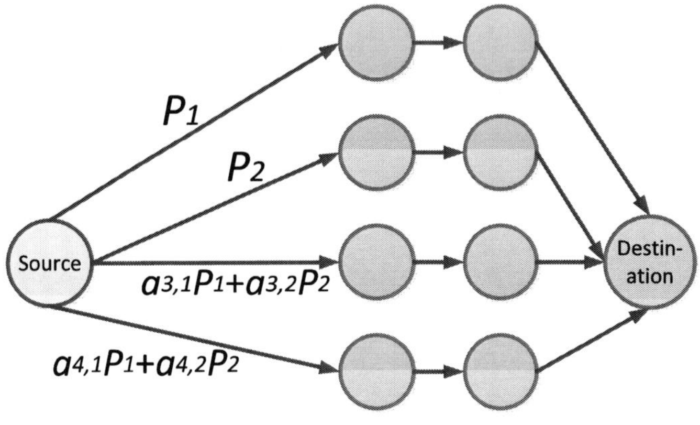

Figure 1. An illustration of the proposed scheme when $D = 4$, $N = 2$, and $M = 2$. Network coding is employed at the source.

to employ network coding at the source. Fig. 1 shows an illustration of the proposed multipath transmission scheme for $D = 4$, $N = 2$, and $M = 2$.

In this chapter, we choose the statistical end-to-end delay as QoS measure, and we denote the random variable $\mathbf{T}_i$ as the end-to-end delay of the ith packet. To support the QoS requirement of the ith packet, $\mathbf{T}_i$ must satisfy the delay constraints such as $\mathbb{P}(\mathbf{T}_i > \tau_i) \leq \epsilon_i$ or $\mathbb{E}[\mathbf{T}_i] \leq \tau_i$, where the former constraint requires that the probability of end-to-end delay exceeding the maximum tolerable delay τ_i must be confined by the outage probability ϵ_i, while the latter constraint requires that the mean end-to-end delay must not exceed the maximum tolerable delay τ_i. The rate R is defined as the fraction of native packets over total transmitted packets, which can be interpreted as the average number of native packets delivered on each path. For repetition based scheme, $R = \frac{N}{N \cdot L} = \frac{1}{L}$. For our proposed scheme, $R = \frac{N}{N+M}$ and it is bounded by

$$\frac{2}{D} \leq R = \frac{N}{N+M} \leq \frac{D-1}{D} \tag{3}$$

due to the constraints $N \geq 2$, $M \geq 1$ and $D - N - M \geq 0$.

If the delay statistics of each path can be evaluated, we are able to find the optimal operating point (N^*, M^*) for rate maximization by solving the optimization problem

$$
\begin{aligned}
\text{Maximize} \quad & R(N, M) \\
\text{Subject to} \quad & Q_i(\mathbf{T}_i),\ 1 \le i \le N, \\
& N \ge 2, \\
& M \ge 1, \\
& D - M - N \ge 0,
\end{aligned} \tag{4}
$$

where $Q_i(\mathbf{T}_i)$ is the QoS requirement of the ith packet in terms of $\mathbb{P}(\mathbf{T}_i > \tau_i) \le \epsilon_i$ or $\mathbb{E}[\mathbf{T}_i] \le \tau_i$.

Fig. 2 illustrates the proposed network coding based multipath transmission scheme and the conventional repetition based scheme. By exploiting network coding at the source, we can create new operating points for rate-delay adaptation and hence enhancing multipath transmission efficiency.

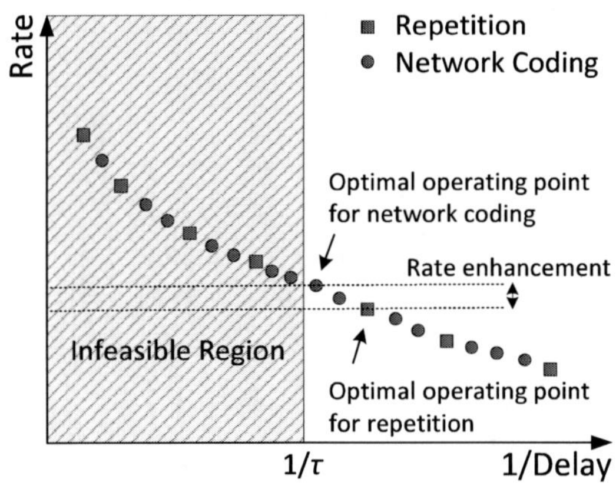

Figure 2. illustration of the proposed network coding based scheme and the conventional repetition based scheme for multipath transmission. The proposed method offers better rate-delay adaptation via network coding by creating new operating points.

3. Analysis of Rate-delay Tradeoffs

We assume the QoS requirements of N native packets are identical ($\tau_i = \tau$ and $\epsilon_i = \epsilon$, $\forall\ i$). Each path consists of multiple hops with retransmission protocol on each hop. Time is divided into discrete time slots and each packet delivery consumes one time slot. Let $\mathbf{Z}_i$ denote the end-to-end delay of the ith path and H_i denote the hop number of the ith path, we have $\mathbf{Z}_i = \sum_{k=1}^{H_i} \mathbf{Y}_{i,k}$, where $\mathbf{Y}_{i,k} \sim \mathrm{GEO}(q_{i,k})$ is a geometric random variable with probability of success $q_{i,k}$ at kth hop of the ith path. Each node keeps forwarding the packet to the next node until the packet is successfully received at the next node. If $\mathbf{Y}_{i,k}$ is an independently and identically distributed (i.i.d) random variable with probability of success q_i, $\mathbf{Z}_i$ follows a negative binomial distribution $\mathrm{NB}(H_i, q_i)$, where the end-to-end transmission is attained with H_i successful receptions. Knowing $\mathbf{Z}_i \geq H_i$, we have the cumulative distribution function (CDF)

$$F_{\mathbf{Z}_i}(z_i) = \sum_{j=H_i}^{z_i} \binom{j-1}{H_i - 1} (1-q_i)^{j-H_i} {q_i}^{H_i} \tag{5}$$

$$= \sum_{j'=0}^{z_i - H_i} \binom{j' + H_i - 1}{j'} (1-q_i)^{j'} {q_i}^{H_i} \tag{6}$$

$$= 1 - I_{1-q_i}(z_i - H_i + 1, H_i), \tag{7}$$

where $I_x(a,b) = \sum_{j=a}^{a+b-1} \frac{(a+b-1)!}{j!(a+b-1-j)!} x^j (1-x)^{a+b-1-j}$ is the regularized incomplete beta function for integer values a and b.

For repetition based scheme, without loss of generality, the end-to-end delay of the first native packet is

$$\mathbf{T}_1 = \min\{\mathbf{Z}_1, \mathbf{Z}_2, \ldots, \mathbf{Z}_L\}. \tag{8}$$

Assuming the delay statistics of L paths are independent, the complementary cumulative distribution function (CCDF) of $\mathbf{T}_1$ becomes

$$\bar{F}_{\mathbf{T}_1}(t) = \mathbb{P}(\mathbf{T}_L > t) \tag{9}$$

$$= \mathbb{P}(\min\{\mathbf{Z}_1,\ \mathbf{Z}_2, \ldots,\ \mathbf{Z}_L\} > t) \tag{10}$$

$$= \mathbb{P}(\mathbf{Z}_1 > t, \mathbf{Z}_2 > t, \ldots, \mathbf{Z}_L > t) \tag{11}$$

$$= \prod_{i=1}^{L} \mathbb{P}(\mathbf{Z}_i > t) \tag{12}$$

$$= \prod_{i=1}^{L} I_{1-q_i}(t - H_i + 1, H_i). \tag{13}$$

Via network coding, the delivery delay of the ith packet utilizing $N+M$ disjoint paths is $\mathbf{T}_i = \min\{\mathbf{Z}_i, \mathbf{Z}_{-i}\}$, where $\mathbf{Z}_{-i}$ is the delivery delay of receiving the first N packets from the other $N+M-1$ paths excluding the ith path. We have

$$F_{\mathbf{Z}_{-i}}(t) = \mathbb{P}(\text{The arriving time of the } N\text{th packet} \leq t) \tag{14}$$

$$= \sum_{j\geq N}^{N+M-1} \sum_{\mathbf{i}\in\Omega_j} \prod_{m=1}^{j} F_{\mathbf{Z}_{i_m}}(t) \prod_{n=j+1}^{N+M-1} \bar{F}_{\mathbf{Z}_{i_n}}(t), \tag{15}$$

where Ω_j is the set of packet arrival events, $\mathbf{i} \triangleq (i_1, \ldots, i_{N+M-1})$ is one realization of arrival path indexes, and the first j components of $\mathbf{i}$ represent the path indexes of the first j packet arrivals with $|\Omega_j| = \binom{N+M-1}{j}$ possible combinations. With (14), the CCDF of $\mathbf{T}_i$ becomes

$$\bar{F}_{\mathbf{T}_i}(t) = \mathbb{P}(\mathbf{T}_i > t) \tag{16}$$

$$= \mathbb{P}(\min\{\mathbf{Z}_i, \mathbf{Z}_{-i}\} > t) \tag{17}$$

$$= \mathbb{P}(\mathbf{Z}_i > t)\mathbb{P}(\mathbf{Z}_{-i} > t) \tag{18}$$

$$= \bar{F}_{\mathbf{Z}_i}(t) \left[1 - \sum_{j\geq N}^{N+M-1} \sum_{\mathbf{i}\in\Omega_j} \prod_{m=1}^{j} F_{\mathbf{Z}_{i_m}}(t) \prod_{n=j+1}^{N+M-1} \bar{F}_{\mathbf{Z}_{i_n}}(t)\right]. \tag{19}$$

If the delay statistics of $N+M$ disjoint paths are i.i.d (i.e., $q_i = q$ and $H_i = H$), by (5), (16) can be simplified as

$$\bar{F}_{\mathbf{T}_i}(t) = \mathbb{P}(\mathbf{T}_i > t) \tag{20}$$

$$= \bar{F}_{\mathbf{Z}_i}(t) - \sum_{j\geq N}^{N+M-1} \binom{N+M-1}{j} [F_{\mathbf{Z}_i}(t)]^j \left[\bar{F}_{\mathbf{Z}_i}(t)\right]^{N+M-j}$$

$$= I_{1-q}(t-H+1, H) - \sum_{j\geq N}^{N+M-1} \binom{N+M-1}{j}$$

$$\times \left[1 - I_{1-q}(t-H+1,H)\right]^j \left[I_{1-q}(t-H+1,H)\right]^{N+M-j}. \tag{21}$$

The mean delivery delay can be evaluated as

$$\mathbb{E}[\mathbf{T}_i] = \sum_{t=\min\{H_i\}}^{\infty} \mathbb{P}(\mathbf{T}_i \geq t). \tag{22}$$

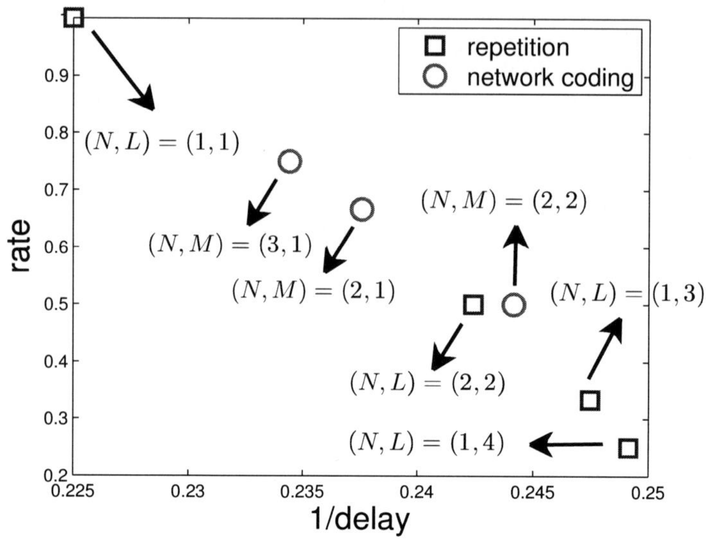

Figure 3. Rate-delay tradeoff points with $D = 4$, $H = 4$ and $q = 0.9$. Network coding based scheme interpolates new tradeoff points for multipath transmissions and reduces the end-to-end delay when the rate is $R = 0.5$.

Consequently, we obtain the rate-delay tradeoffs with respect to the operating point (N, M). Moreover, since $K \triangleq D - M - N$ ranges from 0 to $D - 3$ and N ranges from 2 to $D - K - 1$, the maximum number of tradeoff points (some of them may be overlapped) with network coding based scheme is

$$\sum_{k=0}^{D-3} (D - k - 1 - 2 + 1) = \frac{1}{2}(D - 1)(D - 2). \tag{23}$$

Our scheme therefore provides much more complete rate-delay tradeoffs and is adaptive to QoS requirements by selecting the closest tradeoff point to delay constraint for rate maximization.

4. Performance Evaluation

For demonstration purpose, we assume $H_i = H$, $Q_i(\mathbf{T}_i) = \mathbb{E}[\mathbf{T}_i] \leq \tau$, $\forall\, i$, and the delay statistics of D disjoint paths are i.i.d. with probability of suc-

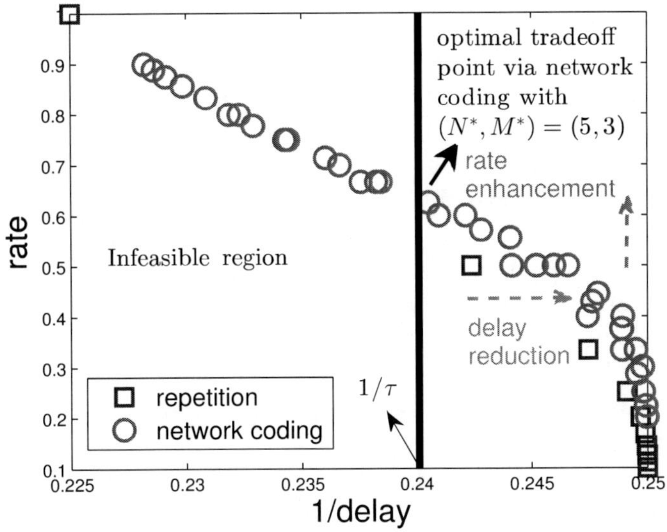

Figure 4. Rate-delay tradeoff points with $D = 10$, $H = 4$ and $q = 0.9$. The maximum tolerable delay is set to be $\tau = 4.17$. The rate can be enhanced from $R = 0.5$ $(L = 2)$ to 0.625 $((N, M) = (5, 3))$ via network coding. Moreover, under the same rate, network coding is able to reduce the end-to-end delay, as long as $R \geq 0.2$.

cess q on each hop. The results are conducted via MATLAB. To clarify the notions of the proposed scheme, we start with $D = 4$ disjoint paths as a motivating example. The rate-delay tradeoff points are shown in Fig. 3. When $R = 1/2$, under repetition based scheme each packet is duplicated and transmitted through two disjoint paths, whereas under our proposed scheme two network-coded packets $\mathcal{P}_3 = a_{3,1}\mathcal{P}_1 + a_{3,2}\mathcal{P}_2$ and $\mathcal{P}_4 = a_{4,1}\mathcal{P}_1 + a_{4,2}\mathcal{P}_2$ are transmitted through path 3 and 4, respectively. The destination is able to decode $\mathcal{P}_i$, $i = 1, 2$, if it receives the data from the ith path, or the data from any two out of other three paths. It is shown that the end-to-end delay can be further reduced via network coding under the same rate. In addition, two new tradeoff points with rates $R = 2/3$ and $R = 3/4$ are created above the rate lower bound $R = 1/2$ for rate adjustment.

In Fig. 4, the maximum tolerable delay is set to be $\tau = 4.17$ with $D = 10$ disjoint paths, and the tradeoff points in the infeasible region fail to support the QoS requirements due to delay violation. Under such a constraint, the maximum achievable rate via repetition based scheme is $R = 1/2$, whereas via our proposed scheme the rate can be enhanced to $R = 5/8$ by setting $N = 5$ and $M = 3$. In other words, given $\tau = 4.17$, the rate can be maximized by choosing the new operating point (N^*, M^*) whose rate-delay tradeoff point is closest to the permissible delay constraint. Moreover, compared with repetition based scheme, the end-to-end delay can be further reduced when $R \geq 0.2$ and $N \geq 2$. Please note that repetition based scheme can still be utilized at extreme cases with stringent delay constraints where the rate is below the lower bound $R = 0.2$. In fact, the tradeoff points created by repetition based scheme are more compact as L grows, which complements our proposed scheme. These two schemes together offer rate-delay tradeoff points with fine granularity for multipath transmissions.

5. Conclusion

A network coding based multipath transmission scheme is proposed to provide profound rate-delay tradeoff points for multipath transmission. Compared with repetition based scheme, our proposed scheme reduces the end-to-end delay and is able to maximize the rate while achieving statistical delay guarantees. Consequently the proposed scheme offers new avenues to rate-delay adaptation in multipath transmission.

Acknowledgment

The author would like to thank Mr. Weng Chon Ao at Department of Electrical Engineering, University of Southern California, Dr. Shin-Ming Cheng at Department of Computer Science and Information Engineering, National Taiwan University of Science and Technology, and Dr. Kwang-Cheng Chen at Department of Electrical Engineering, National Taiwan University, for their valuable discussions.

References

[1] J. Q. Hu, "Diverse routing in optical mesh networks," *IEEE Trans. Commun.*, vol. 51, no. 3, pp. 489–494, Mar. 2003.

[2] R. Irmer, H. Droste, P. Marsch, M. Grieger, G. Fettweis, S. Brueck, H.-P. Mayer, L. Thiele, and V. Jungnickel, "Coordinated multipoint: Concepts, performance, and field trial results," *IEEE Commun. Mag.*, vol. 49, no. 2, pp. 102–111, Feb. 2011.

[3] P.-Y. Chen, S.-M. Cheng, W. C. Ao, and K.-C. Chen, "Multi-path routing with end-to-end statistical QoS provisioning in underlay cognitive radio networks," in *Proc. IEEE INFOCOM Workshops*, Apr. 2011, pp. 1–6.

[4] M. K. Marina and S. R. Das, "On-demand multipath distance vector routing in ad hoc networks," in *Proc. IEEE ICNP*, Nov. 2001, pp. 14–23.

[5] P.-Y. Chen, W. C. Ao, and K.-C. Chen, "Rate-delay enhanced multipath transmission scheme via network coding in multihop networks," *IEEE Commun. Lett.*, vol. 16, no. 3, pp. 281–283, March 2012.

[6] W. C. Ao, P.-Y. Chen, and K.-C. Chen, "Rate-reliability-delay tradeoff of multipath transmission using network coding," *IEEE Trans. Veh. Technol.*, vol. 61, no. 5, pp. 2336–2342, Jun 2012.

[7] P. Djukic and S. Valaee, "Reliable packet transmissions in multipath routed wireless networks," *IEEE Trans. Mobile Comput.*, vol. 5, no. 5, pp. 548–559, May 2006.

[8] S. Fashandi, S. Gharan, and A. Khandani, "Path diversity over packet switched networks: Performance analysis and rate allocation," *IEEE/ACM Trans. Netw.*, vol. 18, no. 5, pp. 1373–1386, Oct. 2010.

[9] R. Ahlswede, N. Cai, S.-Y. Li, and R. Yeung, "Network information flow," *IEEE Trans. Inf. Theory*, vol. 46, no. 4, pp. 1204–1216, July 2000.

[10] R. Koetter and M. Medard, "An algebraic approach to network coding," *IEEE/ACM Trans. Netw.*, vol. 11, no. 5, pp. 782–795, Oct. 2003.

[11] O. Al-Kofahi and A. Kamal, "Network coding-based protection of many-to-one wireless flows," *IEEE J. Sel. Areas Commun.*, vol. 27, no. 5, pp. 797–813, June 2009.

[12] A. Kamal, "1+N network protection for mesh networks: Network coding-based protection using p-cycles," *IEEE/ACM Trans. Netw.*, vol. 18, no. 1, pp. 67–80, Feb. 2010.

[13] X. He and A. Yener, "On the energy-delay trade-off of a two-way relay network," in *Proc. CISS*, Mar. 2008, pp. 865–870.

[14] S. Gharan, S. Fashandi, and A. Khandani, "Diversity-rate trade-off in erasure networks," in *Proc. IEEE INFOCOM*, Mar. 2010, pp. 1–9.

[15] O. Trullols-Cruces, J. Barcelo-Ordinas, and M. Fiore, "Exact decoding probability under random linear network coding," *IEEE Commun. Lett.*, vol. 15, no. 1, pp. 67–69, Jan. 2011.

In: Network Coding and Data Compression ISBN: 978-1-63483-185-7
Editor: MaryAnn Simmons © 2015 Nova Science Publishers, Inc.

Chapter 2

PHYSICAL LAYER NETWORK CODING FOR HETEROGENEOUS WIRELESS NETWORKS

Wasiu Opeyemi Oduola[1,*], ***Xiangfang Li***[1,†], ***Lijun Qian***[1,‡] ***and Deepak Kataria***[2,§]
[1]Electrical and Computer Engineering Department,
Prairie View A& M University,
Texas A& M University System, Prairie View, TX, US
[2]Consulting Director, IP Junction Inc.,
Bridgewater, NJ, US

Abstract

The concept of network coding has emerged as a very promising technique that can be used to improve the efficiency of spectral utilization and systems throughput in wireless communications. In network coding, intermediate nodes or relays mix the information signals they receive and forward the mixture to several destinations simultaneously. Physical-layer Network Coding (PNC) defines a form of network coding which could convert interfering signals to an harmless phenomenon directly from modulated and demodulated signals

*E-mail address: woduola@pvamu.edu
†E-mail address: xili@pvamu.edu
‡E-mail address: liqian@pvamu.edu
§E-mail address: Deepak.kataria@ip-junction.com

at the physical-layer. PNC equally provides a means to eliminate the interference-induced scrambling of signals which results in packet collisions at the medium access control layer of existing wireless networks. This book chapter presents the theory, applications and challenges of a physical-layer network coding technique that promises significant improvement to the spectral efficiency and interference mitigation challenges in future heterogeneous cellular and wireless networks. Specifically, examples of PNC application in Femtocell-Macrocell overlay network are presented. A major challenge with wireless and cellular systems is maintaining a balance between reliable communication and higher spatial reuse of the spectrum. One promising resolution technique is by using femtocells to bring the receiver nearer to the transmitter. A Femtocell-Macrocell overlay network forms an heterogeneous network which significantly improves the indoor coverage and provides better mobile user experience. Interference is generally undesirable in such an heterogeneous network because it causes collisions, corrupts received signals, and wastes limited bandwidth. For instance, in a macrocell-femtocell overlay network, radio frequency interference will result from a macrocell interfering with a femtocell or vice versa and such interference may considerably degrade the performance of the cellular system. Instead of viewing interference as a counterproductive phenomenon that should be avoided, this chapter provides a PNC scheme that transforms interference into a safe and beneficial phenomenon. This is due to the ability of PNC to embrace electromagnetic interference, improve spectral efficiency and achieve throughput optimality, thus making PNC suitable for the heterogeneous cellular network. The book chapter discussed different applications of a PNC scheme that exploits the interference of concurrent transmissions at the femtocell to increase network throughput and mitigate the interference.

1. Introduction

The proliferation of smart phones, tablets, and other data-centric and media-hungry devices is making wireless and mobile systems have increasingly vital roles in the daily lives of mobile subscribers. As a result, mobile subscribers in a cellular system usually have an ever growing demand in terms of high data rate and multimedia requirement, data transfer and high speed download. Such mobile users' demands constantly result in the challenge of maintaining a balance between reliable communication and higher spatial reuse of the spectrum. Also, a study[1] by ABI research showed that in the future, over 50% of voice calls and more than 70% of data traffic is expected to originate from indoor mobile users [2]. To mobile subscribers, this translates to the need for better quality indoor coverage and better indoor voice and data services. This would also be of benefit to service providers in the form of increased revenue. However, it compels service providers to increase the capacity of their networks. To do this in a cost-effective manner, service providers are migrating from the expensive traditional tower-mounted, high-power base stations towards heterogeneous cellular networks [3, 4]. This development presents several opportunities for capacity increase as well as creating new research problems such as interference management, co-existence and network management of the heterogeneous entities.

In existing literatures, there have been different approaches to tackling interference between transmitted signals, such as power control for Home NodeB (HNB) and macrocell users [5], allocating different orthogonal resources to transmitted signals in time, frequency and space [6], or by the removal and cancellation of interferers from the signal of interest if allocating orthogonal resources between the interfering signal and the desired signal is not feasible or economical [6]. However, the above techniques may not guarantee the complete mitigation of the harmful effect of interference in some cases [6, 7, 8] that is, there may not be enough or inexpensive resources to obtain orthogonality among signals, and interference cancellation does not decrease the interference to an acceptable level. Hence, rather than avoiding or suppressing interference resulting from simultaneously transmitted electromagnetic waves (EM waves) due to multiple mobile users, this chapter extends the interference handling ability of physical-layer network coding (PNC) [9, 10, 11] to the heterogeneous macrocell-femtocell network.

1.1. Physical Layer Network Coding for Heterogeneous Networks

Network coding emerged as a promising transmission technique to improve spectral efficiency and system throughput [12] in wireless networks. In network coding, intermediate nodes or relays mix the information signals they receive and forward the mixture to several destinations simultaneously. The

[1]Another survey showed that 30% of business and 45% of household users experience poor indoor coverage [1].

broadcast nature of wireless transmission is ideal for the application of network coding. PNC is a network coding technique that promises significant improvement to the interference mitigation challenge in a two-tier heterogeneous network. Interference is generally undesirable in a cellular network because it causes collisions, corrupts received signals, and wastes limited bandwidth. In a macrocell-femtocell overlay network, radio frequency interference will result from a macrocell interfering with a femtocell or vice versa.

PNC defines a form of network coding [12] which could convert interfering signals to an harmless phenomenon directly from modulated and demodulated signals at the physical-layer. PNC equally provides a means to eliminate the interference-induced scrambling of signals which results in pack-collisions at the medium access control layer protocol of existing wireless networks [9]. The proposed PNC scheme exploits the interference of concurrent transmissions at the HNB to increase network throughput and eliminate interference. The ability of PNC to embrace electromagnetic interference, improve spectral efficiency and achieve throughput optimality makes it suitable for the heterogeneous cellular network.

1.2. Heterogeneous Cellular Networks

Service providers are making a paradigm shift in the deployment of cellular network infrastructure. The carefully planned but expensive traditional tower-mounted, high-power base stations are being migrated towards heterogeneous cellular networks [3, 4]. Heterogeneous cellular networks consists of N spatially coexisting tiers of randomly deployed base stations where one tier is distinguished from the other in terms of size/coverage, transmit power, data rate, signal propagation environment and density of base stations [4, 19]. Example of such heterogeneity is the co-existence of macrocells, microcells, picocells and femtocells which differ based on their area of coverage, transmit power, size, propagation characteristics and the type of back-haul medium [4].

The paradigm shift in cellular network deployment creates several opportunities for increasing the fundamental capacity limit as well as creating new research problems relating to co-existence and network management of the heterogeneous entities. In addition, Chandrasekhar et al. [13] noted that the topology of heterogeneous cellular network challenges many deep-rooted modeling aspects of conventional cellular system modeling and analysis [4]. For instance, it will be an obsolete modeling concept to:

- Use uniform hexagonal grid to model the locations of base station in heterogeneous cellular networks due to the irregular deployment of base stations in such heterogeneous networks.
- Assume that a mobile user should generally connect to the base station providing the strongest received signal strength (RSS) as this is quite often not the one providing the best rate in a heterogeneous cellular network.

Fig. 1 depicts a three-tier heterogeneous network which is made up of a mix of macro, pico and femtocell base stations. Only a single macrocell is shown for the sake of simplicity. As shown in Fig. 1, for instance, traditional base stations or macrocell (tier 1) would typically have a much higher transmit power, size and a lower density than the lower tiers (e.g., pico and femtocells) [20]. The macrocell is the largest tier and it provides the widest coverage area of all the tiers. The macrocell is usually located along major highways or sparsely populated regions. The next smaller size cell is the picocell. It is used in small densely populated urban areas like large office buildings, industrial areas, shopping malls and other commercial areas. The smallest tier in terms of coverage is the femtocell. Femtocells are usually located in homes, offices or hot-spots.

1.2.1. Interference in Heterogeneous Cellular Networks

There are two major types of interference in the heterogeneous (multi-tier) architecture [21, 22]. These are depicted in Fig. 1 and explained as follows:

1) Co-tier Interference: This is the interference caused by user equipments or network entities that belong to the same tier. For example, in the case of femtocells, it is the interference caused by a femtocell to another femtocell. The interfering femtocells are usually neighboring femtocells since they are not far away from each other. This is because femtocells are deployed in a random manner and very close to each other in homes, office buildings or hot-spots. The wall separation might not be enough to prevent the femtocells from interfering with each other. Due to the proximity of the femtocells, there is a high likelihood of power leaks to neighboring

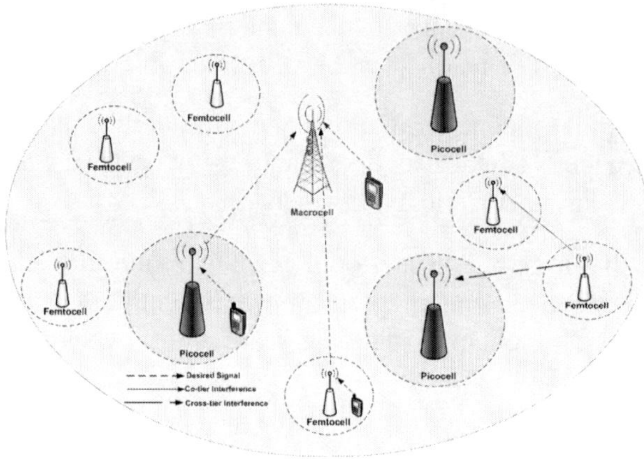

Figure 1. Three-tier heterogenous network consisting of a mix of macro, pico and femtocell base stations.

femtocells through windows, doors and other apertures. These power leaks cause interference to the neighboring femtocells [21, 22].

2) Cross-tier Interference: This is the interference caused by network entities that belong to different tier of the heterogeneous network. For example, an HNB causing interference to the downlink of a nearby MUE or an MUE causing interference at the uplink of a HNB nearby. The cross-tier uplink interference can also occur when a HUE causes interference to the MNB or when a MUE transmits at high power close to a femtocell user causing interference at the downlink transmissions to the HUE. The femtocells are usually isolated as a result of the wall penetration losses, but still in some cases the MUE can be a source of sufficient interference to the femtocell. To mitigate cross-tier interference, separate channel deployment has been proposed. However, this is not an efficient solution as spectrum is expensive and limited. This calls for an efficient interference management technique in same channel deployment [21, 22].

1.3. Overview of Femtocells

A major challenge with cellular systems is maintaining a balance between reliable communication and higher spatial reuse of the spectrum. One promising resolution technique is by using femtocells to bring the receiver nearer to the transmitter [13]. Femtocells are reduced cost and reduced transmit power data access points that works with existing cellular communication system but requires the deployment of a new HNB that uses a licensed frequency band [14]. They are usually installed by consumers or users for the purpose of receiving better indoor voice quality, higher data rate service, improved battery life and so on [35]. A femtocell is linked to the mobile operator's network through the broadband Internet media such as the digital subscriber lines, cable modems, or a separate radio frequency backhaul channel. In current designs, HNBs normally allow less than 5 active HUEs in homes, and up to 16 active HUEs in offices [24]. Femtocells gives service providers the flexibility to extend their service coverage at the cell edge or indoors, especially where access would otherwise be limited or unavailable [25]. For a mobile service provider, the merits of an HNB include improvements to coverage and capacity, especially indoors and highly reduced upfront cost [13]. Consumers benefit from improved coverage and potentially better quality of voice service and better life span of battery. When comparing femtocells with other strategies for improving system's capacity, such as the distributed antenna arrays, and micro-cells, the advantage of HNBs is that the installation and upfront cost to the service provider is very little [13].

Femtocells provide an effective solution for the coverage problem indoors. Specifically, due to reduced cell radius, the transmitter to receiver distance is reduced, hence transmitted information signal is less attenuated and in turn indoor mobile users can receive a better Received Signal Strength (RSS) [25]. Generally, the quality of an information signal received is measured in form of Signals to interference plus noise ratios (SINR). The penetration losses due to obstacles or walls cause the interfering signals from neighboring femtocells to be weak[2]. Thus, femtocells transmit with low power while maintaining good indoor coverage quality [26]. Femtocells are deployed within a macrocell in a random fashion and users can move femtocells from one location to another just like the Wireless Fidelity (Wi-Fi)

[2]Though this assumption may no longer be valid when taking into consideration the sum total of all interfering femtocells at the HNB of interest

access points. Therefore, it becomes a challenging problem for service operators to dynamically manage radio resources [27]. It also requires that the femtocells be efficiently self organising to ensure it has awareness of its environment. The main challenge faced by femtocells is interference management because of their unplanned deployment and closeness to each other. This requires that the femtocells have inherent interference mitigation techniques [28, 26].

Femtocells became more famous in 2005 and the actual term femtocell was coined in 2006 [27]. Afterwards, in July 2007, several vendors, operators and research bodies came together to form a non-profit organisation called Femto Forum [29]. The Femto Forum was created to promote standardization and wide-scale adoption of femtocells. This forum has played a vital role in ensuring that the standards were agreed upon and released to the public. The members list consist of more than one hundred operators and telecoms vendors. The forum is established to provide a good linkage between the new technology and industry. The femtocells became main stream technology when the Third Generation Partnership (3GPP) release 8 introduced the HNB and Home e Node B (H(e)NB) [30]. Future Long Term Evolution (LTE) networks have been predicted to include femtocells for the indoor cellular coverage. Thus, in the not-too distant future, femtocells are likely to be deployed at a large scale [27].

1.3.1. Femtocells Access Modes

Femtocells usually support a limited number of users ranging from two to four active mobile users in homes, and eight to 16 active mobile users in an office environment. Therefore, there is the need to spell out clearly which user can access a specific femtocell. The following are basically the three access modes for a femtocell [32, 33, 34, 23]:

1) Open Access mode: In this mode, every mobile user can connect to the femtocell and benefit from its services. This mode suffers from privacy concerns for privately owned infrastructures as well as increased frequency of handoffs experienced by mobile users [23].

2) Closed Access mode: in this mode, the femtocell only serves specific or registered users. The desirable benefits of closed access includes security, protection of finite backhaul capacity, and the reduction in the frequency of handoffs experienced by mobile users [33].

3) Hybrid Access mode: In this mode of access, access to the femtocell is granted to particular outside users. The conditions of access by an outside user to the femtocell can be defined by each service operator separately and access by any guest or new user can be requested by the owner of the femtocell [32].

The mobile subscribers who install their own femtocells are unlikely to favor open access mode. This is because home users who purchased the HNB and pays for the backhaul would not like to share their femtocell resources with others. However, this mode can be used in public areas like parks, universities, airports and shopping malls to provide better coverage to the users in that area [27]. Home users generally prefer closed access mode, but in this mode, interference from MUEs near the femtocell becomes a challenging problem. Access modes have a direct impact on the interference in the system. One solution technique is the hybrid access mode which provides a more effective solution by allowing certain MUEs to access the resources of a nearby femtocell. However, the number of allowed MUEs has to be carefully defined. This is due to the negative impact that increasing number of permitted MUEs has on the performance of authorized femtocell users.

1.3.2. Deployment Configurations of Femtocell Networks

There are three types of deployment configurations for femtocell networks [36].

1) Orthogonal Deployment: In this configuration, the spectrum is divided into two independent segments. One spectrum is used by the femtocells while the other is used by the macrocells. This approach has the advantage of eliminating inter-tier interference, but the frequency resources are not efficiently utilized.

2) Cochannel Deployment: In cochannel deployment, both femtocells and macrocells have access to all available channels. Such deployment configurations usually generate an excessive level of cochannel interference.

3) Partial Cochannel Deployment: In this deployment configuration, the whole spectrum is divided into two parts, one dedicated to the macrocells and the other shared by macrocells and femtocells [37]. This benefits from the advantages of both orthogonal and cochannel deployments while partly avoiding their short-comings.

2. Network Coding Fundamentals

Network coding emerged as a promising transmission technique at the network layer of the protocol stack to improve the network capacity, spectral efficiency and system throughput [12]. In network coding, intermediate nodes or relays combine the information signals they receive and convey the mixture to several destinations simultaneously. In comparison with time sharing based schemes where destinations are served one after the other, the use of network coding can increase the overall throughput dramatically. The broadcast nature of wireless transmission is ideal for the application of network coding. For instance, when there are multiple simultaneous transmissions to a single intermediate node, the multiple messages will be superimposed at the receiver. Similarly one relay transmission can also be overheard by multiple destinations because of the broadcast nature of wireless medium [39].

As an illustration, consider the conventional butterfly network [40] consisting of source nodes, $S_1 \& S_2$, destination nodes, $D_1 \& D_2$, and intermediate nodes, $R_1 \& R_2$ as shown in Fig. 2. Each source node wants to distribute its packet to a set of destination nodes with the help of the intermediate nodes. For instance, source S_1 wants to deliver packet PKT_1 to both $D_1 \& D_2$, and source S_2 wants to deliver packet PKT_2 to both destinations as well. Assume all links are error free and have limited resources. All links have a unit capacity of one packet per second [41].

In traditional communication networks, the packets are sent from the source nodes through the intermediate nodes to destination nodes by store-and-forward switching [42] as shown in Fig. 2(a). Since the capacity of the link between $R_1 \& R_2$ is one, the relay nodes create a bottleneck in the middle link because for every second, they can either convey PKT_1 to D_2 or PKT_2 to D_1 [41].

In contrast, network coding [12] provides the potential to increase network capacity significantly. The key idea of network coding is to allow an intermediate node to mix and process packets or information signals from multiple nodes [39]. In this way, the amount of information transmitted through the network can be decreased thereby increasing the network throughput.

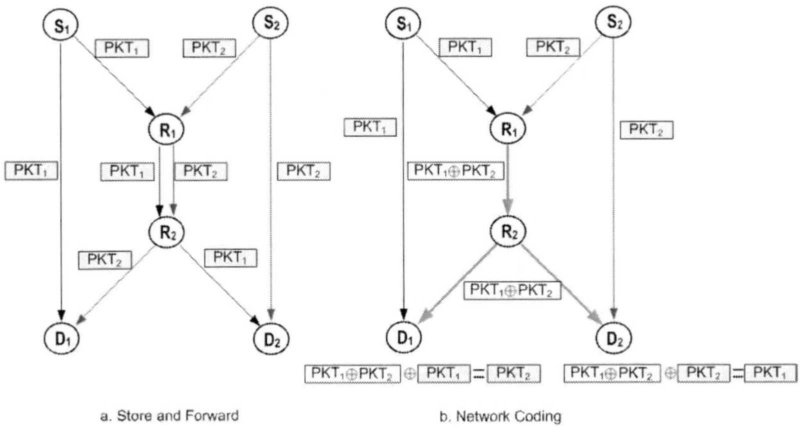

Figure 2. The butterfly network for store and forward versus network coding.

With network coding [12, 39], the bottleneck node R_1 in the middle link computes the exclusive-OR (XOR) of the two packets and sends $PKT_1 \oplus PKT_2$ as shown in Fig. 2(b). How does each destination node obtain both packets ($PKT_1 \& PKT_2$)? Since $D_1(D_2)$ knows both $PKT_1(PKT_2)$ and $PKT_1 \oplus PKT_2$, it can get $PKT_2(PKT_1)$ by XORing packet $PKT_1(PKT_2)$ which it received on the direct link from $S_1(S_2)$ with $PKT_1 \oplus PKT_2$. Thus, network coding saves bandwidth and energy and can obtain a multicast throughput of two packets per second, which is better than the traditional routing approach which can at best achieve 3/2 packets per second [41].

2.1. What Is Physical Layer Network Coding?

Physical-layer network coding (PNC) [9, 10, 11] can further improve the network performance. In PNC, the relay computes the desired network coded information signal from the simultaneously transmitted signals by suitable modulation and demodulation. In a traditional two-way relay transmission scheme as shown in Fig. 3(a), communication can take place over four time slots, where node S_1 transmit its packet PKT_1 to node S_2 through a relay node R in the first two time slots with node S_2 remaining idle. Node S_2 is then allowed to transmit its packet PKT_2 to node S_1 through the relay in the last two time slots with node S_1 remaining idle [11].

The first implementation of PNC in a 2-way relay network (TWRC) using the universal software radio peripheral (USRP) was presented in [43]. The idea behind PNC was proposed concurrently in 2006 by several different groups: Zhang et al. [9], Popovski and Yomo [10] and Nazer et al. [11]. But Zhang et al. came up with the term PNC. Nazer et al. [44] proposed a reliable PNC which employs carefully selected linear error-correction code (ECC), such that relay nodes could straightly retrieve linear functions of the information packets from the superimposed signals transmitted. Popovski et al. proposed the amplify and forward strategy for a TWRC [45]. Interested readers could read surveys [46], [44] and the references therein for more detailed overview and concepts of PNC.

Zhang et al. [9], was inspired by the observation that the relay node R does not need to know the individual contents of the information signals $(PKT_1\&PKT_2)$ from the sources $(S_1\&S_2)$ to transform the superimposed packets received to the network-coded packet $(PKT_1 \oplus PKT_2)$ for broadcast to the terminal points. The needed information could be obtained even if the two end nodes were to transmit simultaneously to the relay in the same time slot [46]. In this way, the number of time slots needed to exchange one packet is reduced to two time slots as shown in Fig. 3(b).

2.1.1. Comparisons of Transmissions with and without PNC

In a traditional system, HUEs and MUEs are not allowed to transmit simultaneously due to the undesirable uplink co-channel interference at HNB. As a consequence, with time sharing, a traditional system requires three time slots to complete the transmissions from HUE to HNB, from HNB to the backhaul, and from MUE to Macrocell or MNB, as shown in Fig. 4 (a). However, with PNC, the time slots could be reduced to two (Fig. 4 (b)) with the additional benefit of improved performance over traditional schemes, including increased throughput, efficient spectrum usage [72] and interference mitigation (as shown later in this chapter). Fig. 3 schematically depicts the time slot comparison.

The PNC concept could be illustrated easily with the aid of the Two-way relay channel (TWRC) [46] in which a source and destination node exchange information signals through an intermediate relay node. A very good exam-

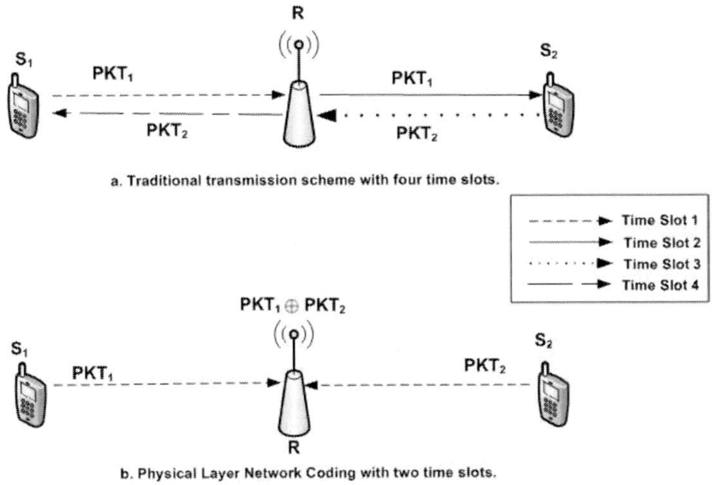

Figure 3. (a). Traditional transmission scheme with four time slots; (b). Physical layer network coding with two time slots.

ple of TWRC is the satellite system where the source and destination are basically ground stations and the intermediate node is the satellite. In such application, PNC allows the end nodes to broadcast their information signals simultaneously and take advantage of the network-coding operation done by nature on superimposed electromagnetic waves. As illustrated in Fig. 3(b), relay node R obtains $P_R = PKT_1 \oplus PKT_2$ in the first time slot. In the second time slot, R transmits P_R to S_1 and S_2. The technique through which R deduces $P_R = PKT_1 \oplus PKT_2$ from the naturally superimposed signals is known as PNC mapping [46].

2.1.2. Application of PNC in Heterogeneous Wireless Networks

PNC is a network coding technique that promises significant improvement to the interference mitigation challenge in a two-tier heterogeneous network. Interference is generally undesirable in a cellular network because it causes collisions, corrupts received signals, and wastes limited bandwidth. When multiple sources transmit concurrently, the information packets collide. However, a closer look at what goes on at the signal level reveals that

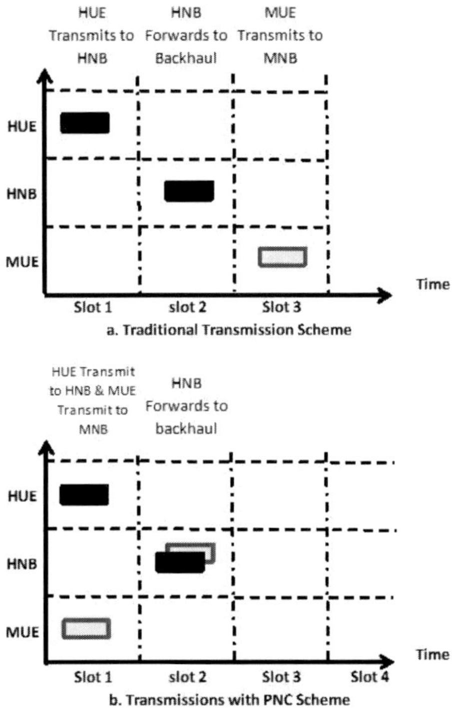

Figure 4. (a). Traditional transmission scheme without network coding; (b). Transmission scheme with physical layer network coding.

such packet collisions simply means that the channel adds their physical signals with attenuations and phase shifts. Thus, after correcting for channel effects, the destination node can recover the desired packet if it knows the content of the packet that interfered with the desired packet. This knowledge provides a basis for the application of PNC to interference mitigation in heterogeneous wireless networks.

In a macrocell-femtocell overlay network, radio frequency interference will result from a macrocell interfering with a femtocell or vice versa. One approach to handling interference between transmitted signals is either by the optimization of the transmission power of both the femtocell and macrocell users [5], establishment of orthogonality between transmitted signals in time, frequency and space [6], or by the active removal and cancellation of interfering signals from the desired signal if orthogonality between the desired signal and potential interferers is not feasible [6]. However, the above techniques may not guarantee the complete mitigation of interference in some cases [6, 7, 8], i.e., there is not enough resources to obtain orthogonality among signals, and interference cancellation does not decrease the interference to an acceptable level. Hence, instead of avoiding or suppressing interference caused by simultaneous electromagnetic waves transmitted from multiple mobile users, this chapter proposed an extension of the interference handling ability of PNC [9] to the heterogeneous macrocell-femtocell network.

The PNC scheme embraces interference to effect network-coding [12] operation directly from physical-layer signal modulation and demodulation. With PNC, signal scrambling due to interference which causes packet collisions in the medium access contro (MAC) layer protocol of traditional wireless networks can be eliminated [9]. The proposed PNC scheme exploits the interference of concurrent transmissions at the HNB to increase network throughput and eliminate interference. The ability of PNC to embrace electromagnetic interference, improve spectral efficiency and achieve throughput optimality makes it suitable for the heterogeneous cellular network.

3. System Models and Problem Formulation

There are several recent works on Physical Layer Network Coding that made it feasible to apply the PNC scheme to interference mitigation in femtocell-Macrocell overlay network. The idea behind PNC was proposed concurrently in 2006 by several different groups: Zhang et al. [9], Popovski and Yomo [10] and Nazer et al. [11]. But Zhang et al. came up with the term PNC. Nazer et al. [44] proposed a reliable PNC which employs carefully selected linear error-correction code (ECC), such that relay nodes could straightly retrieve linear functions of the information packets from the superimposed signals transmitted. Popovski et al. proposed the amplify and forward strategy for a TWRC [45]. Interested readers could read surveys [46, 44] and the references therein for more detailed overview and concepts of PNC.

In [9], the authors noticed that a relay (or HNB) could reduce number of transmission time slots from four to two by converting the superimposed source signals received to the network coded signals for broadcasting to destinations. The intermediate relay is not expected to know the individual components of source packets. The desired packet could be obtained even if the two terminal points transmit concurrently to the intermediate node within same time slot. Also, bit-error rate (BER) is reduced. The first practical implementation of PNC in a two-way relay network using the universal software radio peripheral (USRP) was presented in [43]. The authors in [48] categorized PNC into infinite field PNC (IPNC) and finite field PNC (FPNC). In FPNC, the signals of interest are denoted by a finite field. In IPNC, an infinite field such as a real number is used to denote the signal of interest. Irrespective of whether FPNC or IPNC is used, it is required that a destination node must be able to retrieve the message broadcasted by the source node from the XORed signal transmitted from the intermediate node.

Analog network-coding (ANC) was proposed in [49], which is also based on collision cancellation mechanism but different from PNC in finite-field in that it uses an algorithm for signal-processing using minimum shift key modulation. However, the Bits Error Rate (BER.) of PNC is found to be better than the one for ANC but worse than the one of Quadrature Phase Shift Keying (QPSK) [50]. The ANC which is an example of infinite-field PNC has desirable advantages if the SNR ratio is reasonably high, however, the accumulated noise end-to-end could be counter productive. A promising solution to this problem is reliable PNC which uses the compute and forward (CF) [51] approach to ensure that resulting noise could be eliminated at every stage through suitably designed ECC. The codes in CF are nested lattices based and this allows decoding of linear combinations of the transmitted packets by intermediate nodes. The nodes then simply forward them towards the end nodes. The end nodes can obtain their needed messages provided they have sufficient linear functions of the codewords. In other words, the encoder maps information signals from finite field onto points of a lattice and the decoder retrieve functions of the points of the lattice and map them back to functions over the finite field. The authors in [52] described a time synchronization scheme for PNC that exploits the preambles in frequency domain and time domain for efficient timing-offset estimation.

In [53], the authors studied the Uplink (UL) capacity in overlaid Femtocell-Macrocell networks through the derivation of lower bounds on the per-tier outage probability. Downlink home base station carrier selection, transmit power calibrations and adaptive uplink attenuation at the home base station were proposed as key interference management methods for overcoming the interference caused by nearby macro user in [14]. Femtocell HUE uplink power control [54] and proper downlink power control of HNB [5] were proposed as key requirement to guarantee the quality-of-service of MUEs and femtocell users. The authors in [55] provided a means to statistically characterize the uplink interference in an heterogeneous femtocell network and its impact on the system performance.

In addition, some of the recent works [56, 57, 58] addressed the downlink physical interference in two-tier heterogeneous networks. For example, in [56], the authors derived the probability density function of the Downlink (DL) Signal to Interference Ratio (SIR) for femtocell networks. Although they took into account the shadowing effect, they did not consider the spatial nor the temporal distribution of the cellular users in their analysis. In [57], DL outage probability was derived for the mobile users conditioned on their distances from the MNB. In [58], the performances of a two-tier femtocell network in terms of DL outage probability, under the assumption of poisson spatially- distributed HNBs was studied. The authors in [59] studied the UL interference in two-tier femtocell networks.

In [60], the work investigated the UL capacity in overlaid femtocell/macrocell Code Division Multiple Access (CDMA) systems through the derivation of lower bounds on the per-tier outage probability. In [59], the authors used a hierarchical static geometric model to characterize the UL interference at the femtocells. In [61], the authors presented a statistical characterization of the UL co-channel physical interference, the SIR and the outage probability at the HNBs in two-tier time division multiple access (TDMA) femtocell/macrocell networks. The work took into consideration the wireless environment specificities (shadowing and pathloss), the spatial distribution and the temporal distribution of the HUEs and MUEs. However, none of the previous works considered the application of PNC to interference mitigation in the heterogeneous cellular network. Embracing Interference in such femtocell-macrocell overlay network is made possible through the application of PNC at the HNB. This novel application is the focus of this chapter.

3.1. Case Study I: Mitigating Uplink Interference in Heterogeneous Network with Physical Layer Network Coding

Interference is generally undesirable in a cellular network because it causes collisions, corrupts received signals, and wastes limited bandwidth. In a femtocell network, radio frequency interference will result from a macrocell interfering with a femtocell or vice versa. Instead of avoiding or suppressing interference caused by simultaneous electromagnetic waves transmitted from multiple mobile users, this chapter investigated the extension of the interference handling ability of PNC [9] to the two-tier heterogeneous femtocell network.

The PNC scheme embraces interference to effect network-coding [12] operation directly from physical-layer signal modulation and demodulation. With PNC, signal scrambling due to interference which causes packet collisions in the medium access control layer protocol of traditional wireless networks can be eliminated [9]. The proposed PNC scheme exploits the interference of concurrent transmissions at the HNB to increase network throughput and eliminate interference. The ability of PNC to embrace electromagnetic interference, improve spectral efficiency and achieve throughput optimality makes it suitable for the femtocell network.

A simple illustration of an uplink macrocell-to-femtocell interference scenario at HNB is shown in Fig. 5. In a traditional system, HUEs and MUEs are not permitted to transmit simultaneously due to the undesirable uplink co-channel interference at HNB. With PNC as shown in Fig. 5, femtocell mobile user HUE_1 and macrocell mobile user MUE_1 transmit their packets ($PKT_1 \& PKT_2$) simultaneously, allowing their transmissions to interfere at the HNB. This consumes a single time slot. The HNB receives a combination of both modulated packets, $PKT_1 \& PKT_2$, the HNB does not necessarily have to decode the bits. The HNB simply uses PNC to exploit the additive nature of simultaneously arriving electromagnetic wave for equivalent network coding operation, and forward $PKT_1 \oplus PKT_2$ to the backhaul. This consumes a second time slot. Since the backhaul already has a copy of PKT_2 which it received from the MNB in the first transmission from MUE_1, it can therefore take the XOR of the signal PKT_2 with the received interfered signal $PKT_1 \oplus PKT_2$, from which it can decode HUE_1's packet.

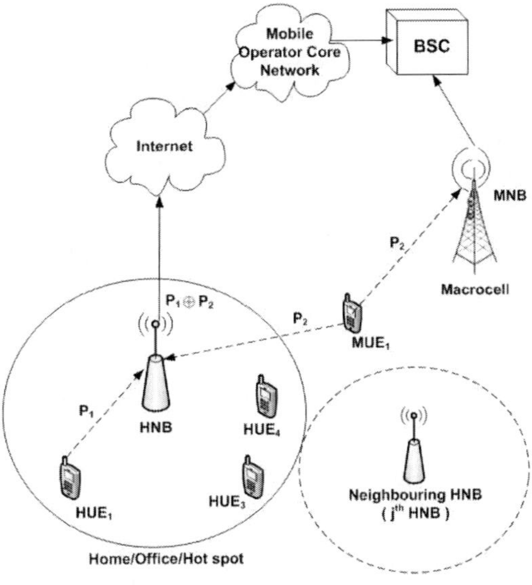

Figure 5. Physical-layer network coding in femtocell network.

3.1.1. Outage Probability of PNC in Femtocell Network

Given an existing MNB, this section stochastically model HUE's and MUE's spatial distributions by independent and homogeneous Poisson Point Processes (PPP), Φ_F and Φ_M, with intensities λ_F and λ_M respectively. This study follows the terms as specified in 3GPP TSG-RAN-WR4 [30]. D is the distance from an MUE of interest to the MNB. The Femtocell's coverage area is a disk with radius l_F while the macrocell's coverage area spans a radius of l_M and $l_M \gg l_F$. Femtocell i supports N_i (usually $N_i \leq 4$) HUEs for data service and voice under its area of coverage. The MUE is d_m meters away from HNB. The total number of HNBs or femtocells is N_F. The transmission powers of the ith HUE is $p_{i,HUE}$, for the mth MUE is $p_{m,MUE}$. The jth HNB's transmission power is $p_{j,HNB}$, with upper limit $p_{HNB}^{max} = 20$ dBm [31]. The distances from the ith HUE and the jth HNB to the HNB of interest are h_i and r_j, respectively (see Fig. 6).

Consider a typical HNB as shown in Fig. 6, this section considered the closed subscriber group (CSG) *uplink co-channel interference mitigation with PNC* when Femtocell and Macrocell are sharing same spectral resources. In Open access, HNBs can serve any UE in the same way as a normal NodeB; while in CSG, HNBs only serve HUEs which are a member of a particular CSG. In dedicated channel deployment, HNBs operate in their own separate channel while in co-channel deployment, HNBs share a channel with an existing Universal Terrestrial Radio Access Network (UTRAN) network [5]. The desirable benefits of CSG include security, protection of finite backhaul capacity and the reduction in the frequency of handoffs experienced by mobile users. For the model, the deployment configurations are CSG and co-channel with the assumption that the HNB is able to perform a PNC operation on unregistered UEs (i.e., MUEs) since the HNB does not have to decode the signals from such unregistered MUEs. Specifically, in a traditional heterogeneous network, the uplink transmissions from the MUEs will normally cause strong interference at a nearby HNB and may cause the received signal at the HNB degraded and become unacceptable [5]. This strong interference is mitigated by using physical layer network coding at the HNB. Hence, the co-channel interference, which is one of the major barriers for the successful co-existence of Macrocell and Femtocell, is transformed to an harmless phenomena through PNC. Based on the established model, the analytical results on the SINR at the HNB and the corresponding outage probability were derived.

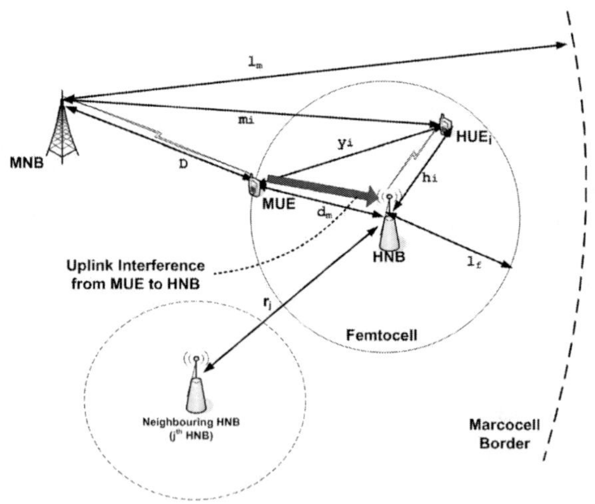

Figure 6. Geometric layout of the macrocell-femtocell overlay network.

3.1.2. The Signal-to-Interference-Plus-Noise Ratio

For a PPP with intensity λ, the probability of n nodes being inside a region R depends only on the total area A_R of R and is given by:

$$P(n \in R) = \frac{(\lambda A_R)^n}{n} \exp(-\lambda A_R) \tag{1}$$

Here λ is the spatial density of the nodes (λ_F for HUEs and λ_M for MUEs in this model), in nodes per unit area. Synchronization is assumed for the uplink (UL) transmissions from the UEs to the HNB [52]. The HNB determines which pair of HUE and MUE to schedule for PNC in a round robin fashion [62]. We assume non-overlapping femtocells and that different time slots are allocated to HUEs within the same HNB, as a result, such HUEs do not interfere with each other.

With the PPP assumption about node locations, the HNB was considered to be situated at the center of a disk of radius l_F representing the area covered by the HNB. Since PNC is used for a pair of HUE and MUE, then the signal at HNB emanates from active HUE and MUE situated in annuli R_1& R_2 respectively and confined by the radii l_F, h_i and l_F, d_m respectively (with respect to the center of HNB). h_i and d_m are selected such that the signal strength due to HUEs beyond h_i is insignificant (similar for the MUEs). In the analysis, it was assumed that the physical channel gain is represented by a combination of pathloss and log-normal shadowing.

For a statistical characterization of the SINR in the heterogeneous network, this section first determines its average and variance, based on PPP properties. Afterwards, its probability density function (PDF) and cumulative distribution function (CDF) are obtained. Let the total signal strength at HNB due to PNC be represented as:

$$E_{HNB} = \sum_{i \in \Phi_F} \frac{\Psi_i P_{HUE}}{h_i^{\alpha_1}} + \sum_{m \in \Phi_M} \frac{\Psi_m P_{MUE}}{d_m^{\alpha_2}} \tag{2}$$

where α_1 and α_2 represent the pathloss exponents due to the HUEs and MUEs, respectively, and $\alpha_2 > \alpha_1 > 2$. P_{HUE} denotes the transmission power of the HUEs, Ψ_i is the amplitude of log-normal shadowing in relation to user i, and the MUE is d_m meters away from the HNB. All nodes are assumed to have a constant transmit power. Hence, $\Psi_i P_{HUE}$ and $\Psi_m P_{MUE}$ are independent log-normal random variables (RVs) It was further assumed that $\Psi_i P_{HUE}$ and $\Psi_m P_{MUE}$ are independent and distributed identically with average μ_1 and μ_2 and variances σ_1^2 and σ_2^2, respectively.

The SINR at the HNB normalized with respect to the additive noise power is given by:

$$\gamma_{HNB} = \frac{E_{HNB}}{\sum_{j \neq i}(p_{j,HNB}/r_j^{\alpha_1}) + \sigma_N^2} \tag{3}$$

where $\sum_{j \neq i}(p_{j,HNB}/r_j^{\alpha_1})$ is the intercell interference at HNB due to the j neighboring femtocells and σ_N^2 is the additive noise power. Since $l_M \gg l_F$, in terms of MNB and the rest j femtocells, the femtocell i and its users can be seen as a point. Therefore, the distance r_j between femtocell i user and femtocell j $(j \neq i)$ can be seen as the distance between the two femtocells.

Intercell HUE to HNB Interference: The interference from neighboring femtocells to HNB is assumed to be negligible compared to other interferences for two reasons:

- The transmit power of HUEs is very low due to the limited range of femtocells.
- After penetrating through multiple walls to reach the femtocell HNB of interest, the signal leakage becomes much weaker.

During UL transmissions, interference caused by an MUE situated at/near the edge of MNB's coverage area may cause the SINR received at the nearby HNB to be below the requirement. For the sake of the analysis in this section, we examined the worst-case scenario in which the MUE is at the femtocell's edge. It could be argued that due to the reasons above, received power at the HNB due to the transmission from MUE will be far greater than the intercell interference generated by neighboring femtocells. This is in addition to the assumption that the femtocells do not overlap and such intercell interference could be ignored with respect to P_{MUE}. An interference limited network is assumed where thermal noise is negligible compared with self-interference.

The UL interference at the HNB was characterized by deriving its first-order and second-order statistics, plus its PDF and CDF as inspired by [55]. The chapter considered the spatial and temporal distribution of the HUEs and MUEs as well as the wireless environment properties, that is, pathloss and shadowing.

The received SINR is given by

$$\gamma_{HNB} \approx \sum_{i \in \Phi_F} \frac{\Psi_i P_{HUE}}{h_i^{\alpha_1}} + \sum_{m \in \Phi_M} \frac{\Psi_m P_{MUE}}{d_m^{\alpha_2}} \tag{4}$$

Proposition 1. *The average, μ, and the variance, σ^2, of the received SINR at HNB can be expressed as:*

$$\begin{aligned} \mu &= \frac{2\pi\lambda_F}{\alpha_1 - 2}\mu_1 \left(\frac{1}{l_F^{\alpha_1 - 2}} - \frac{1}{h_i^{\alpha_1 - 2}} \right) \\ &+ \frac{2\pi\lambda_M}{\alpha_2 - 2}\mu_2 \left(\frac{1}{l_F^{\alpha_2 - 2}} - \frac{1}{d_m^{\alpha_2 - 2}} \right) \end{aligned} \tag{5}$$

$$\begin{aligned} \sigma^2 &= \frac{\pi\lambda_F}{\alpha_1 - 1}(\sigma_1^2 + \mu_1^2) \left(\frac{1}{l_F^{2(\alpha_1 - 1)}} - \frac{1}{h_i^{2(\alpha_1 - 1)}} \right) \\ &+ \frac{\pi\lambda_M}{\alpha_2 - 1}(\sigma_2^2 + \mu_2^2) \left(\frac{1}{l_F^{2(\alpha_2 - 1)}} - \frac{1}{d_m^{2(\alpha_2 - 1)}} \right) \end{aligned} \tag{6}$$

Proof. see Appendix [16].

3.1.3. Outage Probability Analysis

This section obtains the closed-form expression for the outage probability performance of the interference mitigating PNC model. Outage probability is a key performance measure in cellular communications. Outage probability is commonly defined as the probability that the SINR of a received signal is below a given threshold (say γ^{tar}). In other words, the signal is assumed to be correctly received when the equivalent received SINR is greater than or equal to the threshold SINR, and the receiver declares an outage when the received SINR is below the threshold SINR. Outage probability is given by the cumulative distribution function (CDF) of the output signal to noise ratio,

$$P_{out} = P_r(\gamma_{HNB} < \gamma^{tar}) \tag{7}$$

To derive an exact closed-form outage probability expression for the PNC scheme, it was observed that γ_{HNB} is equivalent to the summation of log-normal RVs that are independent. Invoking the help of Fenton-Wilkinson approximations [63] for distribution of the summation of such log-normal RV, the equivalent SINR (γ_{HNB}) is the log-normal RV characterized with the PDF:

$$f(\gamma) = \frac{1}{\sqrt{2\pi}\gamma\sigma_o} \exp\left(\frac{-(\ln\gamma - \mu_o)^2}{2\sigma_o^2}\right) \tag{8}$$

where $\mu_o = \ln\left(\frac{\mu^2}{\sqrt{\mu^2+\sigma^2}}\right)$ and $\sigma_o^2 = \ln\left(\frac{\mu^2+\sigma^2}{\mu^2}\right)$

Also, from the PDF, the CDF was obtained as [24]:

$$P_{out} = F(\gamma) = \frac{1}{2} erfc\left[\frac{-(\ln\gamma^{tar} - \mu_o)}{\sigma_o\sqrt{2}}\right] \tag{9}$$

where $erfc(.)$ is the complementary error function.

3.1.4. Simulation Results

In this section, the performances of the PNC scheme proposed is examined. We considered that $N = 500$ concurrently active HNBs were overlaid with the macrocell within a 1000×1000 meter squared area, sharing the same spectral resources. MNB is situated at the area's central part and MUE of interest is situated near the macrocell's border ($D = 500$ m). The Femtocell's location is 2-D distributed uniformly with all Femtocells within 10×10 squared meter home. None among all the Femtocells are overlapping. The HNB's location is 2-D distributed uniformly in every Femtocell. HUEs are within 10 meters away their respective HNBs and the location is distributed uniformly. Fig. 7 depicts a sample deployment scenarios. The remaining simulations parameters is tabulated as shown on Table 3.1. As shown in Fig. 8, the outage probability for the proposed PNC scheme outperforms the traditional scheme. When the desired outage probability is 10^{-3}, the gain is about 6 dB.

Finally, in Fig. 9, the behavior of the outage probability as a function of the spatial density (nodes per unit area) of femtocell under PNC is illustrated for different Macrocell spatial densities. This curve is vital since it constrains the allowable density and consequently the number of active HUEs in the underlying Macrocell to meet a desired quality of service or value of the outage probability. For example, in order to maintain the outage probability at the HNB $P_{out} \leq 0.1$, the spatial density of active HUEs in the Macrocell should be approximately 0.17 for a MUE density of 0.1.

Table 1. Simulation parameters

Parameters	Value
p_{MNB}	40 dBm
p_{HNB}	variable
p_{HUE}^{max}	20 dBm
p_{MUE}^{max}	20 dBm
σ^2	10^{-14}
D	500 m
l_F	10 m
α_1	2.5
α_2	4.0
λ_F	0.15
λ_M	0.01
γ^{tar}	0.05 dB
σ_1	3.5 dB
σ_2	6.5 dB

3.2. Case Study II: Femtocell as a Relay with Application of PNC

Elkourdi et al. [15] explored the possibility of operating the femtocell access points as relays with the decoder of both MUE and HUE at the mobile operator network. The authors studied the advantages of this approach by developing an outage analysis over quasi-static fading channels in the uplink transmission. The work showed that in the CSG approach, the overall performance loss due to the presence of additional indoor users in the femtocell can be overcome if the HNB is used as relay. The authors in [64] and [65] considered interference avoidance and mitigation techniques in cellular system design as a means to reduce the overall interference. The authors in [66] focussed on relaying in LTE advanced for the indoor environment using amplify and forward relaying for indoor coverage extension. A wireless relay is placed inside a building to compensate for the penetration loss caused by the walls of the building.

End-to-end performance of wireless systems with relays over rayleigh fading channels and derivation of closed-form expressions for the statistics

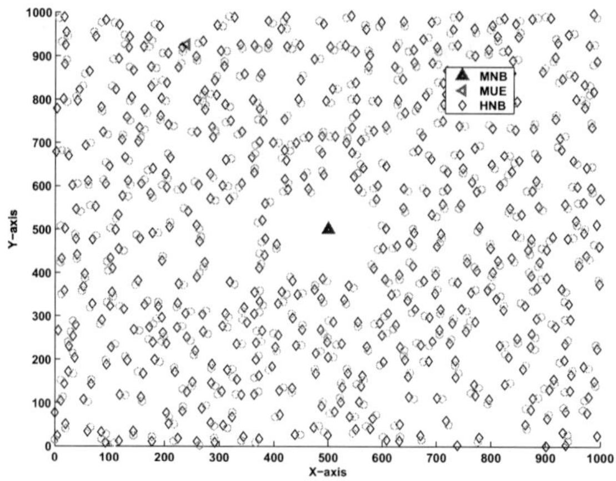

Figure 7. An example deployment of femtocells overlaid with a macrocell.

of the harmonic mean of two independent exponential variates was the focus of [67]. Downlink HNB carrier selection, TX power calibrations and adaptive uplink attenuation at the HNB were proposed in [14] as key interference management methods for overcoming interference caused by nearby MUE. This section considers implementing PNC at the HNB relay in order to nullify the interfering signals from the MUEs. This section looks at the application of PNC for uplink interference nullification in the context of femtocells operating as a relay. The application of PNC in femtocell as a relay enables interference to be viewed as an harmless and beneficial phenomenon. The objective of this chapter is to study a new method to view and mitigate interference in a femtocell operated as a relay. The proposed solution is based on the application of PNC at the femtocell-relay access point to nullify the intefering signals from the MUE. Also, the outage performance of PNC in such a femtocell-relay set up is investigated.

3.2.1. Femtocell as a Relay

Femtocells gets the receiver closer to the transmitter [13] to get better indoor voice and higher data rate service [35]. Femtocells use a licensed spectrum [14]. The HNB connects to the service operators core network through digital subscriber lines (DSL), optical fibre or cable broadband connection. HNBs could also use other wireless technologies like Wi-Fi for the purpose

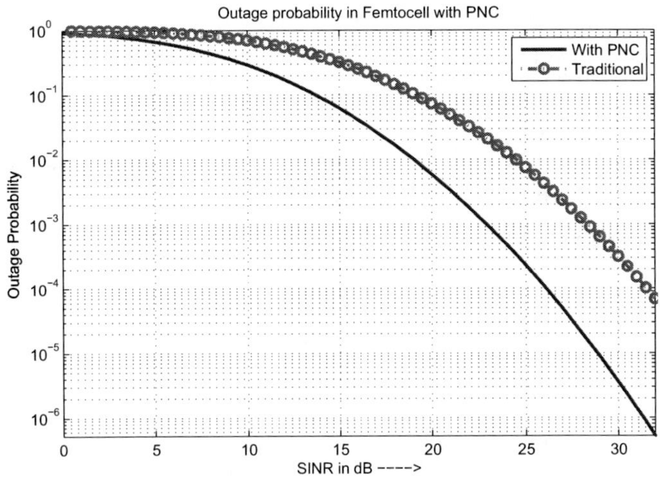

Figure 8. The outage probability versus signal to noise ratio.

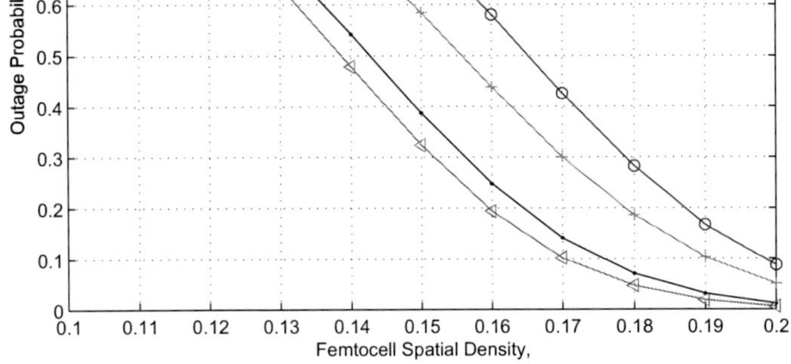

Figure 9. The outage probability as a function of the femtocell spatial density.

of connecting to the backhaul. In cases where there are no broadband connections (e.g., rural areas), a satellite Internet connection might also be used. For a mobile operator, the attractions of a femtocell are improvements to both coverage and capacity, especially indoors and very little upfront cost [13]. Consumers benefit from improved coverage and potentially better voice quality and battery life.

Conventional designs typically stipulates that the HNB acts as an independent encoder and decoder supporting two to four active mobile users in homes and eight to 16 active mobile users in an office environment. However, in [15], the authors explored the possibility of operating the HNBs as relays with the decoder of both Macrocell User Equipment (MUE) and Home User Equipment (HUE) at the mobile operator network. In this sense, the HNB can be used as a relay to provide *soft* information regarding the received signal to the decoder in order to facilitate decoding.

Relay transmission schemes offer significant performance benefits, including being able to achieve spatial diversity through node cooperation [68] and increasing coverage with little transmission powers. This makes relays choice options to be used in cellular, wireless and military communications [69].

3.3. Common Relaying Protocols

The two most common relaying protocols are:

1) Decode and Forward: In Decode and Forward (DF) relaying protocol, the relay node digitally decodes, and re-encodes the source information before re-transmitting it to the destination node. This reduces the overall noise level.

2) Amplify and Forward: The Amplify and Forward (AF) protocol is a form of relaying scheme that amplifies the signal transmitted from the source and forwards it to the destination with no decoding performed at the relay. In this case, the received signal could be a disrupted one due to noise and fading and this may result into a reduction in the channel capacity.

There are several other existing relaying protocols in the body of literature such as the compute and forward relaying, compress and forward relaying [44]. In addition, variations of cooperative relaying techniques include incremental, opportunistic, fixed-gain and variable-gain relaying strategies which are implemented based on the number of actively participating nodes in the information relaying process and whether the channel state information (CSI) is available or not.

In this section, the AF relaying protocol is considered. Operating femtocells as relays may potentially compensate for the performance losses resulting from the presence of other active users in the cell and even provide overall performance gains as well as improve transmission reliability for HUEs and MUEs [15]. This approach enables cooperative communications between HNB and Macrocell NodeB (MNB).

The performance of PNC in a femtocell operating as relay is evaluated. Motivated by [15], it was shown that the use of PNC in such a femtocell-relay system has interference mitigation capability in addition to the potential to improve network throughput and spectral efficiency of the relay based femtocell network.

3.3.1. Physical Layer Network Coding in Femtocell Relays

In a femtocell network, RF interference will result from a macrocell interfering with a femtocell or vice versa. However, with PNC, signal scrambling due to interference, which causes packet collisions in the MAC layer protocol of conventional wireless networks can be eliminated [9]. PNC is known to embrace interference to effect network-coding [12] operation directly from physical-layer signal modulation and demodulation. The PNC-HNB-relay scheme proposed in this study exploits the interference of concurrent transmissions at the HNB to increase network throughput and eliminate interfering signals from both MUEs and HUEs. This is made possible due to the ability of PNC to embrace electromagnetic interference, improve spectral efficiency and achieve throughput optimality. A brief illustration of PNC in a femtocell-relay is depicted in Fig. 10 and Fig. 11. This work focusses on the *uplink* transmissions. With time sharing, a traditional femtocell relay system requires four time slots to complete the transmissions from both HUE and MUE to HNB and from the HNB to the backhaul as shown in Fig. 11a. However, with PNC, as shown in Fig. 10, the HUE and MUE simultaneously transmit their packets, PKT_1 and PKT_2, to the HNB-relay during the first time slot. The HNB-relay receives a combination of both modulated packets, performs equivalent PNC operation then amplifies and forwards the XOR of

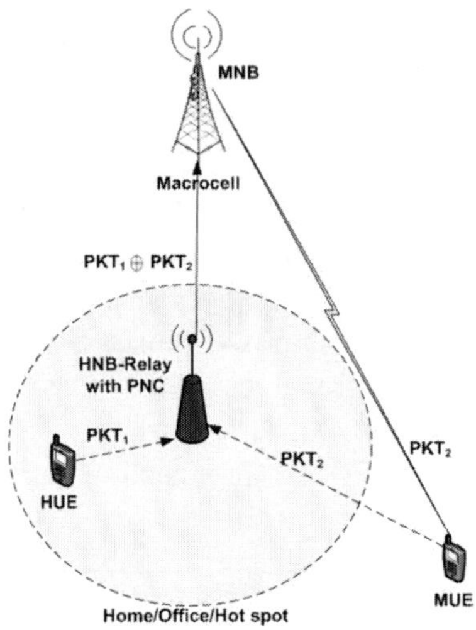

Figure 10. Physical layer network coding in femtocell-relay network.

the two signals, $PKT_1 \oplus PKT_2$ to MNB through the backhaul within the second time slot. Since MNB knows the signal, PKT_2, that MUE transmitted in the first time slot, it can take the XOR of the signal PKT_2 with the received interfered signal, $PKT_1 \oplus PKT_2$ making it possible to decode HUE's and MUE's packets. Thus the number of time slots is reduced to two (Fig. 11b) with the additional benefit of improved performance over traditional schemes, increased throughput and efficient spectrum usage [72].

3.3.2. System Model for a Femtocell Relay

Given an existing MNB with transmission (TX) power p_{MNB}. The TX powers of the HUE, MUE and HNB-relay are p_{HUE}, p_{MUE} and p_{HNB}, respectively, with $p_{HNB}^{max} = 20$ dBm [31]. The performance advantage of PNC in an Open Subscriber Group (OSG) co-channel deployment of HNB-relay was investigated. Specifically, this section focuses on the interference mitigation on the uplink using PNC. In open access, HNBs can serve any UE like a normal NodeB, in Closed Subscriber Group(CSG), HNBs only serve UEs which are members of a CSG. In co-channel deployment HNBs share channel with a UTRAN [5] unlike in dedicated channel deployment. Benefits of OSG are

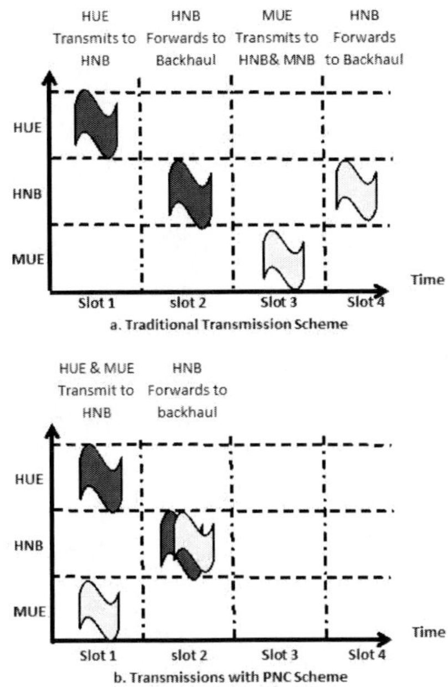

Figure 11. (a) Traditional relay transmissions without network coding; (b). Transmission scheme with physical layer network coding.

the unrestricted access of an MUE to any femtocell with the best received signal strength and the alleviation of cross-tier interference between UEs [70]. However, the strong interference due to the co-existence of macrocells and femtocells may degrade the received signal transmitted from the HUE and MUE [5]. In this work, this interference is mitigated by implementing PNC at the HNB-relay.

The HNB-relay to the MNB link is a broadband link with capacity in bits per channel use [15]. Subscripts 1, 2, H and M denote HUE, MUE, HNB and MNB respectively. h_{ij} is the Rayleigh fading of link i to j. The forward and backward channels are assumed to be reciprocal, i.e., $h_{ij} = h_{ji}$. The complex noise associated with each node is modeled as an independent AWGN with zero mean and variance N_0 denoted as $n_i \sim \text{CN}\ (0, N_0)$. The HNB relay and decoder are assumed to obtain accurate estimates of the link fading coefficients through training sequences in the protocol headers [71] and the femtocell relay is assumed to share link information with the decoder. HUEs and MUE simultaneously transmit their signals, say X_1 and X_2 in a round robin fashion to HNB. The received signal at HNB-relay is:

$$Y_H = \sqrt{P}h_{1H}X_1 + \sqrt{P}h_{2H}X_2 + n_H \tag{10}$$

It was assumed that $p_{HUE} = p_{MUE} = P$. During the second time slot, The HNB-relay forwards Y_H (i.e., $PKT_1 \oplus PKT_2$ in Fig. 10) to the MNB. Since the MNB knows the transmitted signal from MUE, it then eliminates the interference term by taking the XOR of $PKT_1 \oplus PKT_2$ and PKT_2 from which HUE's packet is decoded. Equivalently, the received signal is:

$$Y' = \alpha_H h_{HM} Y_H + n_1 = \alpha_H \sqrt{P} h_{HM} h_{1H} X_1 + \alpha_H \sqrt{P} h_{HM} h_{2H} X_2 + \alpha_H h_{HM} n_H + n_M \tag{11}$$

where α_H is the amplifying gain at the HNB relay. After the elimination of the interference term ($\alpha_H \sqrt{P} h_{HM} h_{2H} X_2$), the resulting signal is decoded as:

$$Y = \alpha_H \sqrt{P} h_{HM} h_{1H} X_1 + \alpha_H h_{HM} n_H + n_M \tag{12}$$

In a traditional system, if there are more than one transmission over the same link, the signals interfere and the receiver cannot decode any of them. However, with PNC, these mixed signals are similar to the output of a relay node after XOR in the network coding system. For simplicity, the focus is on the signal to noise ratio (SNR) of the received signal which is given as:

$$SNR = \frac{P\alpha_H^2 h_{HM}^2 h_{1H}^2}{\alpha_H^2 h_{HM}^2 N_0 + N_0} \tag{13}$$

Set $h_1 = |h_{1H}|^2$, $h_2 = |h_{2H}|^2$ and $h_3 = |h_{HM}|^2$, where h_1, h_2 and h_3 are independent exponentially distributed random variables with parameters λ_1, λ_2 and λ_3 respectively. The received SNR is obtained as:

$$SNR = \frac{\alpha_H^2 \beta h_1 h_3}{\alpha_H^2 h_3 + 1} \tag{14}$$

where $\beta = \dfrac{P}{N_0}$ and one choice of α_H is given in [71, 47] as:

$$\alpha_H = \sqrt{\frac{\beta}{\beta h_1 + \beta h_2 + 1}} \tag{15}$$

3.3.3. Outage Probability Analysis for Femtocell as a Relay

To evaluate the performance advantages of PNC in HNBs operating as relays in the uplink, we derived a closed-form expression for the outage probability of the PNC-HNB-relay model by following the approach in [67]. Outage probability is a key performance measure in cellular communications. It is commonly defined as the probability that the SNR of a received signal is below a given threshold (say γ^{tar}). The receiver declares an outage when the received SNR is below γ^{tar}. Outage probability is given by the cumulative distribution function (CDF) of the output SNR:

$$P_{out} = P_r(SNR < \gamma^{tar}) \tag{16}$$

The following proposition provides a closed-form expression of the outage probability for the PNC HNB-relay scheme.

Proposition 2. *For the PNC in femtocell relay scheme, an exact closed-form outage probability expression is given by:*

$$P_{out} = \int_0^{\gamma^{tar}} f(h)\,\mathrm{d}h = F(\gamma^{tar}) = 1 - 2\sqrt{\frac{\gamma^{tar}}{\alpha_H^2\beta}}K_1\left(2\sqrt{\frac{\gamma^{tar}}{\alpha_H^2\beta}}\right)\exp\left(\frac{-\gamma^{tar}}{\beta}\right) \tag{17}$$

where $K_1(.)$ is the first order modified Bessel function of the second kind, $f(h)$ is the probability density function (PDF) of the SNR and $F(\gamma^{tar})$ is the corresponding CDF.

Proof. see Appendix [17].
For high SNR regime, the following approximation holds: Considering

$$\lim_{x\to 0} xK(x) = 1$$

$$P_{out} \sim 1 - \exp\left(\frac{-\gamma^{tar}}{\beta}\right) \tag{18}$$

3.3.4. Simulation Results

Simulation results are presented here to show the performance of the proposed PNC in femtocell relay. It is assumed that 1000 simultaneously active Femtocells are overlaid with a macrocell in a 2000 X 2000 squared meter area

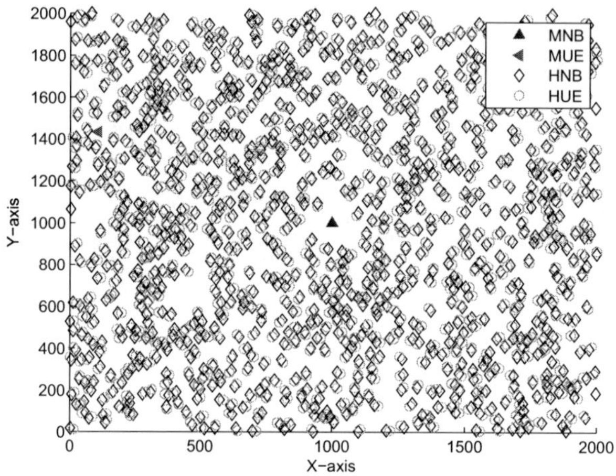

Figure 12. An example deployment of femtocells overlaid with a macrocell in femtocell as a relay setup.

sharing the same spectrum. The MNB is located at the center of the area. The location of the Femtocell is 2-D uniformly distributed and none of the Femtocells are overlapping. The HUE's location is uniformly distributed with respect to its corresponding HNB. Fig. 12 shows an example deployment scenario. Fig. 13 compares the outage performance against SNR for femtocell operated as a relay with and without PNC. The proposed PNC scheme provides approximately 5dB gain over the traditional scheme. In addition, the simulated outage probability matches with the exact outage probability obtained by the expression derived. Fig. 14 shows the mean spectral efficiency obtained with PNC and with time sharing. It shows that with PNC, we can achieve an higher spectral efficiency as compared with the traditional transmission scheme.

4. Discussions and Open Problems

Zhang et al. [9], was inspired by the observation that the relay node does not need to know the individual contents of the information signals from the sources to transform the superimposed packets received to the network-coded packet for broadcast to the terminal points. The needed information

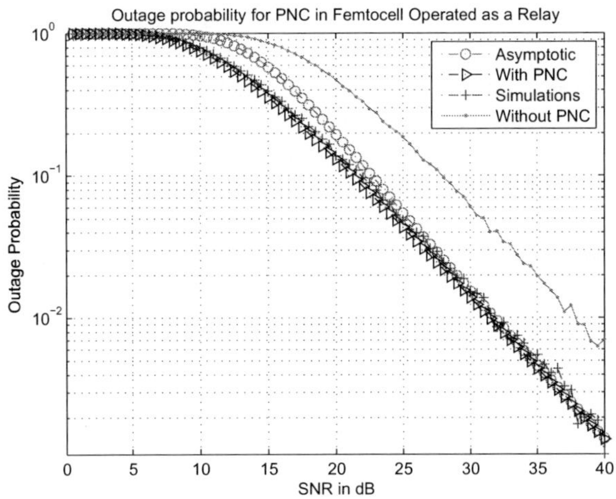

Figure 13. Outage probability for PNC in femtocell operated as a relay.

could be obtained even if the two end nodes were to transmit simultaneously to the relay in the same time slot. PNC simply exploits this concept to treat interfering signals at the physical layer as a beneficial phenomenon. Heterogeneous wireless and sensor networks gives rise to numerous opportunities for applying physical layer network coding. However, they are also associated with vast and diverse challenging problems that demands the attention of the research community.

The simplified case studies on PNC applications presented in this chapter opens up many theoretically relevant questions as well as challenges in PNC implementation in a practical and realistic context. An interesting question might be how to determine the performance of this approach when deployed? Given an arbitrary network topology, what would be the achievable rate of this method over such network? How can the coding be done in a more practical sense with diverse interference scenarios?. It should also be noted that assuring the right superpositions of the various signals at the intermediate nodes requires that the transmitting nodes be synchronized. This is made more challenging because, in practice, timing might be affected by propagation delays, channel conditions, differences in processing times and clock skews. Although, there are research works on asynchronous PNC but our understanding of the asynchrony in PNC is not as thorough as those of synchronous PNC.

Thus, deploying PNC in practice will demand certain additional resources for synchronizations and added capabilities for all the nodes in the system which may include storage services and the ability to perform operations over finite fields. Furthermore, new architectures and protocols might have to be designed or the existing ones might have to be adapted for heterogeneous wireless networks such that PNC capabilities are activated. The aforementioned thus calls for an assurance that we are not incurring unbearable complexities in the deployment of PNC in practice.

This research on the application of physical layer network coding to heterogeneous wireless network and femocell relays opens up several other interesting research areas that can be investigated and that may provide an insight into our understanding of the open problems in this area and the best approach to tackle them. Research studies to consider may include : the design and implementation of a prototype PNC-HNB hardware and comparing the performance with existing HNBs in real life context; application of PNC to data aggregation in mission critical wireless sensor networks ; developing a generalized PNC model for heterogeneous cellular network over myriads of fading channels like Nakagami, rice channels and so on; investigating the application of PNC to other heterogeneous wireless ad-hoc networks and cyber-physical systems such as the advanced metering infrastructure in smart grid; developing a unified analytical framework to understand the performance of PNC in a multiple HNB set up as well as multiple femtocell relay scenario.

5. Conclusion

This book chapter presents the theory, applications and challenges of a physical layer network coding technique that promises significant improvement to the spectral efficiency and interference mitigation challenge in future heterogeneous cellular or wireless networks. Specifically, the chapter investigates the outage performance of a femtocell network that employs physical layer network coding (PNC) to guarantee the QoS of macrocell users and femtocell users by taking advantage of both the signals from MUE and HUE, rather than considering the signal from the MUE as interference. In this sense, applying PNC at HNB eliminates the interference between femtocell users and macrocell users. The first case study developed the exact closed-form expres-

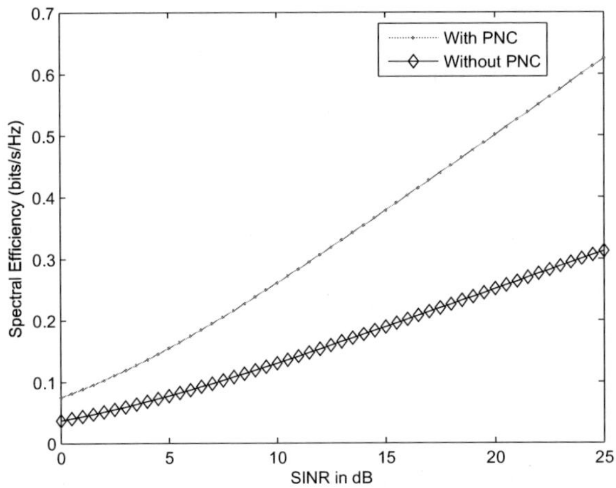

Figure 14. Average spectral efficiency for PNC in femtocell operated as a relay.

sion for the outage probability of the proposed scheme and showed that utilizing PNC at the HNB converted the generated interference by a macrocell user to useful signal for PNC. The proposed scheme is especially effective when the MUE is located at the edge of the coverage area of the MNB, in which case without PNC the signal from the MUE could cause the received SINR at the nearby HNB to fall below the required threshold in the CSG uplink communication and cause outages.

In addition, we examine the outage performance of femtocell as a relay which utilizes PNC to guarantee the QoS of mobile users through the elimination of interference between HUEs and MUEs in the uplink. The second case study evaluated the performance of the scheme and showed that the use of PNC in such a femtocell-relay system converted the interference between mobile users to a harmless phenomenon. This is in addition to improving spectral efficiency (i.e., using less time slots) of the femtocell-relay network. The PNC scheme takes advantage of signals from both HUEs and MUEs rather than considering the signal from the MUE as interference. The case study equally obtained the exact closed-form expression for the outage probability and the simulation results showed that PNC is suitable for the femtocell operated as a relay. Operating femtocells as relays enables cooperative communications between HNB and MNB. This also has the potential to compensate for the performance losses resulting from the presence of other active mobile users in the cell and provides overall improvement in transmission reliability of HUEs and MUEs.

Acknowledgment

This research study is sponsored partly through the US Army Research Office (Cooperative Agreement W911NF-12-1-0054).

References

[1] Cullen, J.: *Radioframe Presentation.* Femtocell Europe, London, UK. 2008, pp. 293-311.

[2] Presentations by ABI Reseach, Picochip, Airvana, IP Access, Gartner, Telefonica Espana, *2nd Intl. Conf. Home Access Points and Femtocells*; Available at: [Online]. http://www.avrenevents.com/dallasfemto2007/purchase presentations.htm .

[3] Dhillon, H.S.; Ganti, R.K.: Baccelli, F.: Andrews, J.G.: Modeling and Analysis of K-Tier Downlink Heterogeneous Cellular Networks. *Selected Areas in Communications, IEEE Journal on*, 2012, vol. 30, no. 3, pp. 550-560.

[4] Ghosh, A.; Mangalvedhe, N.: Ratasuk, R.: Mondal, B.: Cudak, M.: Visotsky, E.: Thomas, T.A.: Andrews, J.G.: Xia, P.: Jo, H-S.: Dhillon, H.S.: Novlan, T.D.: Heterogeneous Cellular Networks: From Theory to Practice. *Communications Magazine*, IEEE, 2012, vol. 50, no. 6, pp. 54-64.

[5] Li, X.; Qian, L.: Kataria, D.: Downlink Power Control in Co-channel Macrocell Femtocell Overlay. *Info. Sc. and Sys, CISS. 43rd Annual Conference on*, 2009.

[6] Boudreau, G.; Panicker, J.: Guo, N.: Chang, R.: Wang , N.: Vrzic, S.: Interference coordination and cancellation for 4G networks. *Coms. Magazine*, IEEE. 2009, vol. 47, no. 4, pp. 74 -81.

[7] Weber, S.P.; Andrews, J.G.: Yang, X.: de Veciana, G.: Transmission Capacity of Wireless Ad Hoc Networks With Successive Interference Cancellation. *Info. Theory, IEEE Trans on*. 2007, vol. 53, no. 8, pp. 2799 -2814.

[8] Andrews, J.G.; Choi, W.: Heath, R.W.: Overcoming interference in spatial multiplexing MIMO cellular networks. *Wireless Communications, IEEE*. 2007, vol. 14, no. 6, pp. 95 -104.

[9] Zhang, S.; Liew, S.C.: Lam, P.: *Hot topic: physical-layer network coding.* MobiCom'06, 2006, pp. 358-365.

[10] Popovski, P.; Yomo, H.: *The Anti-Packets Can Increase the Achievable Throughput of a Wireless Multi-Hop Network.* IEEE ICC, 2006, pp. 3885-3890.

[11] Nazer, B.; Gastpar, M.: Computing over Multiple-Access Channels with Connections to Wireless Network Coding. *Info. Theory*, 2006 *IEEE Intl. Symp. on*, 2006, pp. 1354-1358.

[12] Ahlswede, R.; Ning, C.: Li, S.-Y.R.: Yeung, R.W.: Network information flow. *Info. Theory, IEEE Trans. on*, 2000, vol. 46, no. 4, pp. 1204 -1216.

[13] Chandrasekhar, V.; Andrews, J.: Gatherer, A.: Femtocell networks: a survey. *Communications Magazine, IEEE*, 2008, vol. 46, no. 9, pp. 59-67.

[14] Yavuz, M.; Meshkati, F.: Nanda, S.: Pokhariyal, A.: Johnson, N.: Raghothaman, B.: Richardson, A.: Interference management and performance analysis of UMTS/HSPA+ femtocells. *Communications Magazine, IEEE*, 2009, vol. 47, no. 9, pp. 102 -109.

[15] Elkourdi, T. ; Simeone, O.: Femtocell as a Relay: An Outage Analysis. *Wireless Coms., IEEE Trans. on* 2011, vol. 10, no. 12, pp. 4204 -4213.

[16] Oduola, W.O.; Qian, L.: Li, X.: Kataria, D.: *Mitigating Uplink Interference in Femtocell Networks with Physical Layer Network coding.* IEEE ANTS, 2013, pp. 1-6.

[17] Oduola, W.O.; Qian, L.: Li, X.: *Femtocell as a Relay with Application of Physical Layer Network Coding.* 11th IEEE CCNC, 2014, pp. 513-518.

[18] Oduola, W.O.; Li, X.: Qian, L.: Han, Z.: *Power Control for Device-to-Device Communications as an Underlay to Cellular System.* IEEE ICC, 2014, pp. 5257-5262.

[19] Dhillon, H.S.; Ganti, R.K.: Andrews, J.G.: Load-Aware Modeling and Analysis of Heterogeneous Cellular Networks. *Wireless Coms., IEEE Trans. on*, 2013, vol. 12, no. 4, pp. 1666-1677.

[20] Dhillon, H.S.; Ganti, R.K.: Andrews, J.G.: *A tractable framework for coverage and outage in heterogeneous cellular networks.* ITA Workshop, 2011, pp. 1-6.

[21] Chandrasekhar, V.; Andrews, J.G.: *Uplink Capacity and Interference Avoidance for Two-Tier Cellular Networks.* GLOBECOM., IEEE. 2007, pp. 3322-3326.

[22] Gulati, K.; Evans, B.L.: Andrews, J.G.: Tinsley, K.R.: Statistics of Co-Channel Interference in a Field of Poisson and Poisson-Poisson Clustered Interferers. *Signal Proc., IEEE Trans. on*. 2010, vol. 58, no. 12, pp. 6207-6222.

[23] Xia,P.; Chandrasekhar, V.: Andrews, J.G.: *Femtocell Access Control in the TDMA/OFDMA Uplink.* IEEE GLOBECOM. 2010, pp. 1-5.

[24] *Log-normal Probability Distribution.* Available at.: [Online]. http://en.wikipedia.org/wiki/Log-normal_distribution. Accessed: December, 2012.

[25] Chandrasekhar, V.; Kountouris, M.: Andrews, J.G.: Coverage in multi-antenna two-tier networks. *Wireless Coms., IEEE Trans. on*. 2009, vol. 8, no. 10, pp. 5314-5327.

[26] Chandrasekhar, V.; Andrews, J.G.: Muharemovict, T.: Zukang, S.: Gatherer, A: Power control in two-tier femtocell networks. *Wireless Coms.*, IEEE Trans. on. 2009, vol. 8, no. 8, pp. 4316-4328.

[27] Zahir, T.; Arshad, K.: Nakata, A.: Moessner, K.: Interference Management in Femtocells. *Communications Surveys Tutorials, IEEE*, 2013, vol. 15, no. 1, pp. 293-311.

[28] Chandrasekhar, V.; Andrews, J.G.: Uplink capacity and interference avoidance for two-tier femtocell networks. *Wireless Coms., IEEE Trans. on*. 2009, vol. 8, no. 7, pp. 3498-3509.

[29] *Femto Forum*, http://www.femtoforum.org/femto/. 2007.

[30] *3GPP TR 25.820, "3G Home NodeB Study Item Technical Report (Release 8)", v8.1.0.*

[31] *Report of the 3GPP TSG RAN WG4 meeting # 47bis.* 2008.

[32] Xia, P; Chandrasekhar, V.: Andrews, J.G.: Open vs. Closed Access Femtocells in the Uplink. *Wireless Coms., IEEE Trans. on*. 2010, vol. 9, no. 12, pp. 3798-3809.

[33] Jo, H.; Xia, P.: Andrews, J.G.: *Downlink Femtocell Networks: Open or Closed?.* IEEE ICC. 2011, pp. 1-5.

[34] Chandrasekhar, V.; Andrews, J.G.: Spectrum allocation in tiered cellular networks. *Wireless Coms., IEEE Trans. on*. 2009, vol. 57, no. 10, pp. 3059-3068.

[35] Xia, P.; Chandrasekhar, V.: Andrews, J.G.: *Femtocell Access Control in the TDMA/OFDMA Uplink.* IEEE GLOBECOM. 2010, pp. 1-5.

[36] Chandrasekhar, V.; Andrews, J.G.: Spectrum allocation in tiered cellular networks. *Communications, IEEE Trans. on*, 2009, vol. 57, no. 10, pp. 3059-3068.

[37] Neruda, M.; Vrana, J.: Bestak, R.: *Femtocells in 3G Mobile Networks.* IWSSIP'09. 16th Intl Conf. on, 2009, pp. 1-4.

[38] Hasan, S. F.; Siddique, N. H.: Chakraborty, S.: Femtocell versus Wi Fi- A survey and comparison of architecture and performance. 1st *International Conference on Wireless Communication, Vehicular Technology, Information Theory and Aerospace and Electronic Systems Technology*, 2009, pp. 916 - 920.

[39] Yeung, R.W.: Network Coding: A Historical Perspective. *Proceedings of the IEEE.* 2011, vol. 99, no. 3, pp. 366-371.

[40] Iwama, K.: Classic and quantum network coding. *8th Intl. Symp. ISPAN.* 2005.

[41] Chen, L.: Butterfly Channel. *Intl. Symp. on Network Coding*, 2011, pp. 1-4.

[42] Kuo, W.; Wang, C.: Two-Flow Capacity Region Of The COPE Principle For Wireless Butterfly Networks with Broadcast Erasure Channels. *Info. Theory., IEEE Trans. on.* 2013, vol. 59, no. 11, pp. 7553-7575.

[43] Lu,L.; Wang, T.: Liew, S.C.: Zhang, S.: *Implementation of physical-layer network coding.* IEEE ICC, 2012, pp. 4734 -4740.

[44] Nazer, B. ; Gastpar, M.: Reliable Physical Layer Network Coding. *Proceedings of the IEEE*, 2011, vol. 99, no. 3, pp. 438-460.

[45] Popovski, P.; Yomo, H.: *Bi-directional Amplification of Throughput in a Wireless Multi-Hop Network.* VTC 2006-Spring. IEEE 63rd , 2006, pp. 588-593.

[46] Liew, S.C.; Zhang, S.: Lu, L.: Physical-layer network coding: Tutorial, survey, and beyond. In *Phys. Commununication*, 2011,pp. 1-58.

[47] Louie, R.: Li, Y.: Vucetic, B.: Practical physical layer network coding for two-way relay channels: performance analysis and comparison. *Wireless Com., IEEE Trans. on*, 2010, vol. 9, no. 2, pp. 764-777.

[48] Zhang, S.; Liew, S.C.: Lu, L.: Physical Layer Network Coding Schemes over Finite and Infinite Fields. *IEEE GLOBECOM*, 2008, pp. 1-6.

[49] Katti, S.; Gollakota, S.: Katabi, D.: Embracing wireless interference: analog network coding. *SIGCOMM Comput. Commun. Rev.*, 2007, vol. 37, no. 4, pp. 397–408.

[50] Hu, P.; Ibnkahla, M.: A survey of physical-layer network coding in wireless networks. *Communications (QBSC)*, 25th Biennial Symp. on, 2010, pp. 311 -314.

[51] Nazer, B.; Gastpar, M.: Compute-and-Forward: Harnessing Interference Through Structured Codes. *Info. Theory, IEEE Trans on*, 2011, vol. 57, no. 10, pp. 6463-6486.

[52] Chang, S.; Kelley, B.: An Efficient Time Synchronization Scheme for Broadband Two-Way Relaying Networks Based on Physical-Layer Network Coding. *Coms Letters*, IEEE, 2012, vol. 16, no. 9, pp. 1416 -1419.

[53] Chandrasekhar, V.; Andrews, J.G.: *Uplink Capacity and Interference Avoidance for Two-Tier Cellular Networks.* GLOBECOM '07. IEEE. 2007, pp. 3322 -3326.

[54] Han, Q.; Guan, X.: Ma, K.: Liu, Z.: *Uplink Dead Zone analysis for co-channel two-tier femtocell network.* WCICA, 10th World Congress on, 2012, pp. 991 -995.

[55] Chakchouk, N.; Hamdaoui, B.: *Statistical characterization of uplink interference in two-tier co-channel femtocell networks.* IWCMC, 8th Intl, 2012, pp. 968 -973.

[56] Sung, K.; Haas, H.: McLaughlin, S.: A semianalytical PDF of downlink SINR for femtocell networks. *Journal on Wireless Coms and Net.*, EURASIP, 2010.

[57] Chu, X.; Wu, J.Y.: Wang, H.: *Outage Probability Analysis for Collocated Spectrum-Sharing Macrocell and Femtocells.* ICC'11, IEEE Intl Conf. on, 2011, pp. 1-5.

[58] Kim, Y.; Lee, S.: Hong, D.: Performance Analysis of Two-Tier Femtocell Networks with Outage Constraints. *Wireless Coms., IEEE Trans. on*, 2010, vol. 9, no. 9, pp. 2695-2700.

[59] Shi, Z.; Wang, H.: Zhao, M.: Reed, M.C.: An uplink analytical model for two-tiered 3G femtocell networks. *Modeling and Optimization in Mobile, Ad Hoc and Wireless Networks (WiOpt), 2010 Proceedings of the 8th International Symposium on*, 2010, pp. 367-372.

[60] Chandrasekhar, V.; Andrews, J.G.: Uplink capacity and interference avoidance for two-tier femtocell networks. *Wireless Coms, IEEE Trans. on*, 2009, vol. 8, no. 7, pp. 3498-3509.

[61] Chakchouk, N.; Hamdaoui, B.: *Statistical characterization of uplink interference in two-tier co-channel femtocell networks.* IWCMC'12, 8th Intl, 2012, pp. 968-973.

[62] Jeon, Y.; Kim, Y.: Park, M.: Lee, I.: *Opportunistic Scheduling for Three-Way Relay Systems with Physical Layer Network Coding.* VTC Spring '11, 73rd IEEE, 2011, pp. 1-5.

[63] Fenton, L.: The Sum of Log-Normal Probability Distributions in Scatter Transmission Systems. *Coms. Sys., IEE Trans on*, 1960, vol. 8, no. 1, pp. 57 -67.

[64] Schrenk, G.L.: *Interference management in cellular system design.* VTC' 84, 34th IEEE, 1984, pp. 148-155.

[65] Almgren, M.; Bergstrom, L.: Frodigh, M.: Wallstedt, K.: *Channel allocation and power settings in a cellular system with macro and micro cells using the same frequency spectrum.* VTC' 96, 46th IEEE, 1996, pp. 1150-1154.

[66] Wirth, T.; Thiele, L.: Haustein, T.: Braz, O.: Stefanik, J.: *LTE Amplify and Forward Relaying for Indoor Coverage Extension.* VTC' 10-fall, 72nd IEEE, 2010, pp. 1-5.

[67] Hasna, M.O.; Alouini, M.-S.: End-to-end performance of transmission systems with relays over Rayleigh-fading channels. *Wireless Coms*, IEEE Trans. on. 2003, vol. 2, no. 6, pp. 1126 - 1131.

[68] Sendonaris, A.; Erkip, E.: Aazhang, B.: Increasing uplink capacity via user cooperation diversity. *Info. Theory, Proceedings IEEE Intl Symp on*, 1998, pp. 156-161.

[69] Pabst, R.; Walke, B.H.: Schultz, D.C.: Herhold, P.: Yanikomeroglu, H.: Mukherjee, S.: Viswanathan, H.: Lott, M.: Zirwas, W.: Dohler, M.: Aghvami, H.: Falconer, D.D.: Fettweis, G.P.: Relay-based deployment concepts for wireless and mobile broadband radio. *Communications Magazine*, IEEE, 2004, vol. 42, no. 9, pp. 80-89.

[70] Elkourdi, T.; Simeone, O.: Outage and Diversity-Multiplexing Trade-Off Analysis of Closed and Open-Access Femtocells. *GLOBECOM '10*, IEEE 2010, pp. 1-5.

[71] Laneman, J.N.; Wornell, G.W.: Energy-efficient antenna sharing and relaying for wireless networks. *IEEE WCNC.* 2000, pp. 7 -12.

[72] Louie, R.: Li, Y.: Vucetic, B.: Practical physical layer network coding for two-way relay channels: performance analysis and comparison. *Wireless Com., IEEE Trans. on*, 2010, vol. 9, no. 2, pp. 764-777.

[73] Stoyan, D.; Kendall, W.: Mecke,J.: *Stochastic Geometry and its Applications*. John Wiley and Sons: 1995.

[74] Abramowitz, M.; Stegun, I.A.: *Handbook of Mathematical Functions With Formulas, Graphs, and Mathematical Tables* . Dover: 9th ed. New York, 1970.

[75] Roberts, G. E.; Kaufman, H.: *Table of Laplace Transform*. Saunders: Philadelphia, PA, 1966.

In: Network Coding and Data Compression ISBN: 978-1-63483-185-7
Editor: MaryAnn Simmons © 2015 Nova Science Publishers, Inc.

Chapter 3

NETWORK AND DISTRIBUTED TURBO CODING BASED HARQ PROTOCOL FOR WIRELESS BROADCASTING SYSTEM*

Kui Xu*[†]*, Wei Xie, Youyun Xu,
Dongmei Zhang and Wenfeng Ma
College of Communications Engineering,
PLA University of Science and Technology, Nanjing, China

Abstract

Wireless broadcasting systems employ multiple retransmissions to guarantee the correct reception of each packet. Traditional hybrid automatic retransmission request (HARQ) protocol retransmits one packet per slot. Hence, a large amount of retransmissions is required to correctly receive all the packets, which leads to low spectrum efficiency. In this paper, we propose a Network coding and distributed Turbo Coding based type-III HARQ (NTC-HARQ) protocol,

*This work was supported by the Major Research Plan of National Natural Science Foundation of China (No. F010607), National Natural Science Foundation of China (No. 61301165, 61371123), the Jiangsu Province National Science Foundation under Grant (No. BK2012055), China Postdoctoral Science Foundation (No. 2014M552612), Jiangsu Postdoctoral Science Foundation (No. 1401178C), the Jiangsu Province National Science Foundation under Grant (No. BK2011002).

[†]E-mail address: lgdxxukui@126.com (Corresponding author)

including XORing Network Coding Combined (XNCC) retransmission strategy at the access node (AN) and joint network-turbo decoding (JNTD) strategy at the user equipment (UE). Specifically, to reduce the overall number of retransmissions, lost packets of different UEs are network coding (NC) combined at the AN by utilizing XNCC strategy. The soft information of the lost packet at each UE can be recovered from the received network coded retransmission packet by using the proposed XORing soft network decoder. The recovered soft information of the UE's lost packet is combined with the local undecodable soft information of the same packet to form a distributed turbo code. A chase combining based distributed turbo decoder is proposed to perform turbo decoding, which introduces coding gain and improves Packet Error Rate (PER) performance. Theoretical analyses and simulation results show that the average number of transmissions performance of the proposed NTC-HARQ protocol outperforms that of the XNCC base type-I HARQ protocol (XNCC-HARQ), traditional NC based HARQ protocol (NC-HARQ) and JNTD based protocol (NC-JNTD).

Keywords: Wireless Broadcasting System, XORing Network Coding Combined Retransmission, Distributed Turbo Codes, Joint Network and Turbo Decoding

1. Introduction

Next generation broadband wireless access (BWA) networks such as WiMAX and Long Term Evolution (LTE) are expected to provide efficient, affordable and ubiquitous internet access for multimedia data broadcasting applications such as stock price, real-time traffic and weather information, HD digital TV video streaming and video conferencing. To ensure users' satisfaction, the Quality of Service (QoS) provided by BWA networks should be comparable to that of wired data broadcasting networks. Although the QoS framework for the next generation BWA system has been designed to support the requirements of multimedia applications, the inherent error-prone nature of the wireless channel often results in high packet error rate (PER) and hence degrades the system reliability.

To transmit information reliably over wireless channel, many approaches are employed, such as Forward Error Correcting (FEC), Automatic Retransmission reQuest (ARQ) and Hybrid Automatic Retransmission reQuest

(HARQ) [1]. Among these approaches, FEC suffers from low transmission efficiency and ARQ faces large delay and low throughput caused by severe fading channel. HARQ, which combines both FEC and ARQ techniques, can contribute to an efficient utilization of the available resources.

In literatures, there are three types of HARQ: type-I HARQ, type-II HARQ and type-III HARQ [2, 3]. In type-I HARQ, the transmitter requires to retransmit the coded packet until this packet is successfully decoded by the receiver or the maximum retransmission limit is reached. In type-II HARQ, the receiver chase combines the retransmission packet with previous transmission attempts of the same packet to obtain the diversity gain. In type-III HARQ (or incremental redundancy), the bits in the subsequently retransmitted packet (or packets) are FEC-coded differently from those in the first packet. The idea is that the redundancy bits previously punctured out are "incrementally" sent with each retransmitted packet. Theoretical analyses and simulation results in [2] show that type-III HARQ outperforms type-II HARQ on the residual PER and throughput performances, and type-II HARQ outperforms type-I HARQ on the aforementioned performances.

1.1. Motivation and Related Work

HARQ has now become a fundamental tool of BWA networks, as it can significantly improve the reliability of wireless link. However, HARQ still encounters challenge in wireless broadcasting applications. As identical packets are transmitted from one source to all the receivers, it is impossible for each receiver to correctly receive all the packets. Therefore, HARQ may require large amount of retransmissions in broadcasting scenario to ensure the correct reception of all the packets at each receiver, which leads to low bandwidth efficiency. In order to improve the transmission efficiency of the wireless broadcasting system (WBS), recently, network coding (NC) [4, 5, 6, 7, 8, 9, 10, 11, 12] has been applied to wireless broadcasting system. The NC based HARQ strategies can be divided into two categories, i.e., the random linear NC [12, 13, 14, 11, 15] based HARQ and the XORing NC [16, 17, 18, 19, 24, 25, 20, 21, 23, 22] based HARQ.

1.1.1. Random Linear NC Based HARQ

For random linear NC based HARQ, all the lost packets are mixed with random linear NC and sent in each retransmission slot [11, 12, 13, 14, 15]. The receivers can decode all the lost packets only if they have received sufficient number of mixed packets. This kind of retransmission strategy has a greater computational complexity and incurs additional delay, which is unsuitable for delay-sensitive applications. In [11], a random linear NC scheme suitable for burst communications over lossy links, named as symbol-duration increased NC is proposed. In [14], a linear random NC based wireless broadcast retransmission scheme is proposed, in which the source code combines all lost packets to a single one by linear NC for retransmission, and receivers are able to decode the original packets by method of Gaussian elimination when they receive enough coded-packets.

1.1.2. XORing NC Based HARQ

This kind of NC problem is also referred to as ºª® ª·©±Æ ±º problem [16]. In [17], it was shown that the optimal solution of index network coding problem is NP-hard. For XORing NC based HARQ, NC is performed on lost packets which are carefully selected to ensure the decodability at the receiver [18, 19, 24, 20, 21, 23, 22]. The authors in [19] investigated an efficient NC scheme for wireless broadcasting. In [20], an adaptive scheme for packet retransmissions to improve the bandwidth efficiency in wireless multicast broadcast services using a combination of opportunistic and full NC is designed. In [21], a rate-controlled NC scheme, which can effectively reduce the decoding delay of the receiver suffering from a poor channel condition, is proposed for wireless broadcasting system. In [22], the authors consider an application of NC to increase the bandwidth efficiency of reliable broadcast in a wireless network. In [23], by virtue of type-II HARQ method, the authors present two kinds of network coded retransmission protocols without soft combining, and design three chase combining schemes on the network coded packets in very detail for LTE-A eMBMS system. A dual XOR HARQ retransmission scheme for wireless broadcasting is proposed in [24], which introduces an additional XOR operation between two lost packets from the individual receiver.

The above literatures [12, 13, 14, 15, 16, 17, 18, 19, 24, 20, 21, 23, 22] address the problem of NC based retransmission for wireless broadcasting system. Unfortunately, the above techniques are not extended to the case where the NC and channel coding are jointly designed to further improve the bandwidth efficiency of wireless broadcasting system. Meanwhile, the lost packets are XORed without considering the $^{o\,a}$ $Æ^{a}$ of each lost packet. In [27, 25, 26, 28], several HARQ transmission schemes based on NC are proposed for wireless unicast scenario. Instead of retransmitting erroneous packets individually, network coded packet constructed by the XOR of several erroneous packets is transmitted. In order to fully exploit the network coded packet in combination with the previously received erroneous packets, soft combining methods with respect to chase combing and incremental redundancy are developed.

1.2. Contributions

In this paper, a Network coding and distributed Turbo Coding based type-III HARQ protocol (NTC-HARQ), including XORing Network Coding Combined (XNCC) retransmission strategy at the access node (AN) and joint network-turbo decoding (JNTD) strategy at the user equipments (UEs), is proposed to improve the overall system spectrum efficiency. At the AN, lost packets of different UEs are combined by utilizing the XNCC strategy and broadcasted to UEs in a single slot. Specifically, at each UE, the recovered soft information of the lost packet is combined with the local soft information of the same packet to form a distributed turbo code. The proposed chase combining based turbo decoder is employed to perform turbo decoding, which introduces coding gain and improves PER performance. Theoretical analyses and simulation results show that the average number of transmissions (ANTs) performance of the proposed NTC-HARQ protocol is superior to that of the XNCC base type-I HARQ protocol (XNCC-HARQ), traditional NC [16, 17, 18, 19, 20, 21, 22] based type-I HARQ protocol (NC-HARQ [16, 17, 18, 19, 20, 21, 22]) and JNTD based HARQ protocol (NC[16, 17, 18, 19, 20, 21, 22]-JNTD) in severe fading channels.

The organization of this paper is as follows. System model is given in section II. The proposed NTC-HARQ protocol is described in section III. Performance analyses in terms of ANTs, memory requirement and computational complexity for the proposed protocol and some related protocols are given in Section IV. The simulation results are shown in Section V. Some conclusions will be drawn in section VI.

2. System Model and Parameters

We consider a wireless broadcasting system, where a wireless AN[1] broadcasts a frame of λ packets to a set $\mathcal{R} = \{R_1, R_2, \cdots, R_M\}$ of M UEs within its coverage, and the UEs try to receive packets transmitted from BS. BS adopts TDMA protocol to broadcast these packets. During a TDMA slot, only one packet could be transmitted, and we assume that the channel coefficient keeps constant during a TDMA slot, while independent with others in different slots. In total, λ TDMA time slots are needed to broadcast λ data packets, and this λ time slots is referred to as □Æø° ø ¨– ø ª. After decoding packets, UEs send feedback messages to report whether packets have been successfully decoded. After □Æø° ø ¨– ø ª, BS starts Œ¨Æ ± – ø ª, in which the BS retransmits packets and UEs send feedback messages to request retransmission of lost packets until all the packets are correctly received. Hence, the proposed NTC-HARQ protocol includes two phases to ensure reliable reception: □Æø° ø ¨– ø ª and Œ¨Æ ± – ø ª.

2.1. Mathematical Description

2.1.1. Signal Transmission in Broadcast Phase

In the initial □Æø° ø ¨– ø ª, the base station (BS) broadcasts a WBS frame $\mathbf{A}$ consisting of λ information vectors, i.e., $\mathbf{A} = \{\mathbf{a}_1, \mathbf{a}_2, \cdots, \mathbf{a}_\lambda\}$. In the kth time slot of □Æø° ø ¨– ø ª, the information vector $\mathbf{a}_k$ (including FEC bits, cyclic redundancy check (CRC) bits and information bits) is encoded by the recursive systematic convolution (RSC) encoder yielding the codeword $\mathbf{b}_k$ = ŒÕ $(\mathbf{a}_k)$, where ŒÕ $(\cdot)$ denotes the RSC encoder. The code bits $b_k(i)$ are mapped to symbols $x_k(i) \in \mathbb{X}$ of the modulation alphabet $\mathbb{X}$ and broadcasted to UEs[2]. In case of block fading channel, the received signal vector at the lth UE in time slot k can be expressed as

$$\mathbf{y}_{l,k} = h_{l,k}\sqrt{P_s}\mathbf{x}_k + \mathbf{n}_k \tag{1}$$

[1]Such as a base station (BS) in a LTE or WiMAX cell.

[2]Note that in order to present the idea of network coding and distributed turbo coding based type-III HARQ for broadcast transmission clearly, we concentrate on main aspects so that several functional components such as CRC attachment, coding/rate matching, scrambing/interleaving, high-order modulation etc. are not discussed in detail in this paper.

where $\mathbf{x}_k$ denotes the transmitted signal packet and $\mathbf{n}_k$ is the noise vector whose elements are identically independent distributed (i.i.d) zero-mean Gaussian random variables with variance $\sigma_{n_l}^2$. P_s denotes the BS's transmission power. The channel coefficient $h_{l,k}, \forall\{l,k\}$ denotes complex zero-mean circular symmetric Gaussian distributed variable with variance $\sigma_{h_l}^2$, i.e., $h_{l,k} \sim \mathcal{CN}\left(0, \sigma_{h_l}^2\right)$.

After receiving packets, UEs try to decode these packets, and whether a packet is decoded successfully can be determined by calculating the CRC bits attached in the tail of the packet. Specifically, based on the received signal $y_{l,k}(j)$, the Log-Likelihood-Ratios (LLRs) for the participating coded bit $b_k(i)$ can be calculated by the soft demapper [30]

$$\begin{aligned} L_{\langle\ a}\ (b_k(i)) &= \ln \frac{\Pr\left\{ b_k(i) = 0 |\, y_{l,k}(j), \hat{h}_{l,k}\right\}}{\Pr\left\{ b_k(i) = 1 |\, y_{l,k}(j), \hat{h}_{l,k}\right\}} \\ &= \ln \frac{\sum_{x\in\mathbb{X}, b_k(i)=0} \exp\left(-\frac{\left|y_{l,k}(j)-\hat{h}_{l,k}\sqrt{P_s}x\right|^2}{\sigma_{n_l}^2}\right)}{\sum_{x\in\mathbb{X}, b_k(i)=1} \exp\left(-\frac{\left|y_{l,k}(j)-\hat{h}_{l,k}\sqrt{P_s}x\right|^2}{\sigma_{n_l}^2}\right)} \end{aligned} \tag{2}$$

where $\hat{h}_{l,k}$ is the estimate of the channel coefficient $h_{l,k}$ [34]. To calculate the probability of $b_k(i) = 0$ (or $b_k(i) = 1$), all possible symbols $x \in \mathbb{X}$ related to $b_k(i) = 0$ (or $b_k(i) = 1$) need to be considered. After getting the LLRs $L_{\langle\ a}\ (b_k(i))$, the RSC decoding can be done by using the maximum-likelihood decoder or the maximum a posteriori (MAP) decoder [33].

2.1.2. Signal Transmission in Retransmission Phase

In the Œ¨Æ ± – ø ª, different lost packets are NC combined, RSC encoded, modulated and retransmitted by the BS. Let $\mathcal{C}$ denote the ø º ºø·ª ª¨, which is defined as an index set of lost packets that can be XORing NC combined. For the information vector set $\mathbf{A}_{\mathcal{C}} = \{\mathbf{a}_i \mid i \in \mathcal{C}\}$ which are lost by different UEs, the BS combines all the information vectors by using NC, i.e., $\mathbf{a}_{\mathcal{C}} = \mathbf{a}_i \oplus \mathbf{a}_j \oplus \cdots \oplus \mathbf{a}_k$, where $\oplus$ denotes the XOR operator. After the RSC encoding and modulation, the retransmitted packet $\mathbf{x}_{\mathcal{C}}$ can be expressed as

$$\mathbf{x}_{\mathcal{C}} = \text{” ±º}(\mathbf{b}_{\mathcal{C}}) \tag{3}$$

where ” $\pm^{o}(\cdot)$ denotes the modulation operator and $\mathbf{b}_C$ = ŒÕ $(\mathbf{a}_C)$. The received signal vector at the lth UE can be expressed as

$$\mathbf{y}_{l,C} = h_{l,C}\sqrt{P_s}\mathbf{x}_C + \mathbf{n}_C \tag{4}$$

where $\mathbf{n}_C$ is the noise vector whose elements are i.i.d zero-mean Gaussian random variables with variance $\sigma^2_{n_l}$. The coefficient $h_{l,C}, \forall\{l, C\}$ denotes complex zero-mean circular symmetric Gaussian distributed variable with variance $\sigma^2_{h_l}$. We assume that the information vector $\mathbf{a}_i$ is lost at the lth UE. Based on the received NC combined retransmission signal $y_{l,C}(m)$, the LLRs of the participating coded bit $b_i(n)$ can be calculated by the following soft demapper (given in (5) at the top of next page),

$$\begin{aligned} L_{\langle\ a}\left(b_i\left(n\right)\right) &= \mathrm{sign}\left(\hat{x}^m_{C\setminus\{i\}}\left(n\right)\right)\ln\frac{\Pr\left\{b_i\left(n\right)=0\middle|\,y_{l,C}\left(m\right),\hat{h}_{l,C}\right\}}{\Pr\left\{b_i\left(n\right)=1\middle|\,y_{l,C}\left(m\right),\hat{h}_{l,C}\right\}} \\ &= \mathrm{sign}\left(\hat{x}^m_{C\setminus\{i\}}\left(n\right)\right)\ln\frac{\sum_{x\in\mathbb{X},b_i(n)=0}\exp\left(-\frac{\left|y_{l,C}(m)-\hat{h}_{l,C}\sqrt{P_s}x\right|^2}{\sigma^2_{n_l}}\right)}{\sum_{x\in\mathbb{X},b_i(n)=1}\exp\left(-\frac{\left|y_{l,C}(m)-\hat{h}_{l,C}\sqrt{P_s}x\right|^2}{\sigma^2_{n_l}}\right)} \end{aligned} \tag{5}$$

where $\hat{x}^m_{C\setminus\{i\}}(n)$ denotes the relative complement (also termed as set difference) operator, sign$(\cdot)$ denotes the sign function, $\hat{x}^m_{C\setminus\{i\}}(n) = [x_{C\setminus\{i\}}(n)]_m$ denotes the modulated signal portion of $x_{C\setminus\{i\}}(n)$ associated with the coded bit $b_{C\setminus\{i\}}(m)$ and sign$(\hat{x}^m_{C\setminus\{i\}}(n)) \in \{1, -1\}$. We can see from (5) that the soft value of the desired coded bit $b_i(m)$ can be obtained from the received combined signal[3].

2.2. Assumptions

In this paper, we will consider the following assumptions:

- In both initial broadcast and retransmission phases, all the packets have the same fixed length and use the same modulation scheme.

[3] In short, thanks to the linear property of CRC code and RSC code, for example ŒÕ $(\mathbf{a}_i \oplus \mathbf{a}_j \oplus \mathbf{a}_k) = \mathbf{b}_i \oplus \mathbf{b}_j \oplus \mathbf{b}_k = \mathbf{b}_i \oplus$ ŒÕ $(\mathbf{a}_j \oplus \mathbf{a}_k)$. Hence, if the lth UE correctly received packets $\mathbf{a}_j$ and $\mathbf{a}_k$, the soft value of the desired coded bit $b_i(m)$ can easily be obtained by using equation (5) from the received multiple packets network coding combined signal $y_{l,C}(m)$.

- In both initial broadcast and retransmission phases, BS adopts TDMA protocol to broadcast these packets. During a TDMA slot, only one packet could be transmitted. We assume that the channel coefficient keeps constant during a TDMA slot, while independent with others in different slots, i.e., the channel is a block fading channel and $\mathbb{E}[h_{l,k}h^*_{m,n}] = \sigma^2_{h_l}\delta_{l,m}\delta_{k,n}$. $\mathbb{E}[\cdot]$ denotes the expectation, $(\cdot)^*$ denotes the complex conjugate and $\delta_{i,j}$ denotes the Kronecker delta function. Hence, the packet losses at different UEs are uncorrelated. Due to the randomicity of UEs' location, we assume the distributions of channels between BS and different UEs are same, i.e., $\sigma^2_{h_l} = \sigma^2_h, \forall l$.

- The BS knows the instantaneous states of all the packets at each UE. Each UE sends an acknowledgement signal (ACK) whenever the packet is received correctly, or else it sends a negative acknowledgement signal (NAK). For simplicity we assume that all the ACK/NAKs are instantaneous and never lost, i.e., the feedback channel is error free and has no delay. So the BS knows: (a) whether or not a packet is lost and (b) the corresponding UE/UEs of the lost packet.

3. The Proposed NTC-HARQ Protocol

The proposed NTC-HARQ protocol includes two phases to ensure reliable packets reception: □Æø° ø ¨– ø ª and Œ¨Æ ± – ø ª.

- □Æø° ø ¨– ø ª: As illustrated in Fig. 1 (BS side), the BS first attaches FEC bits and CRC bits in the tail of the information vector. Then, BS broadcasts the RSC encoded and modulated packets to UEs. As illustrated in Fig. 1 (UE side), each UE receives packets and tries to decode these packets. Whether a packet is successfully decoded is determined by the CRC attached in the packet tail. Each UE sends a HARQ feedback (ACK/NAK) to the BS after RSC decoding and CRC checking. Specifically, each UE sends an ACK signal whenever the packet is received correctly, or else it sends a NAK signal. If the received signal is decodable (CRC checking is correct), the correctly received information vector (output of RSC decoder) will be stored in the packet buffer. Otherwise, if CRC checking is wrong, the soft information vector (output of soft demodulator) will be stored in the soft information buffer.

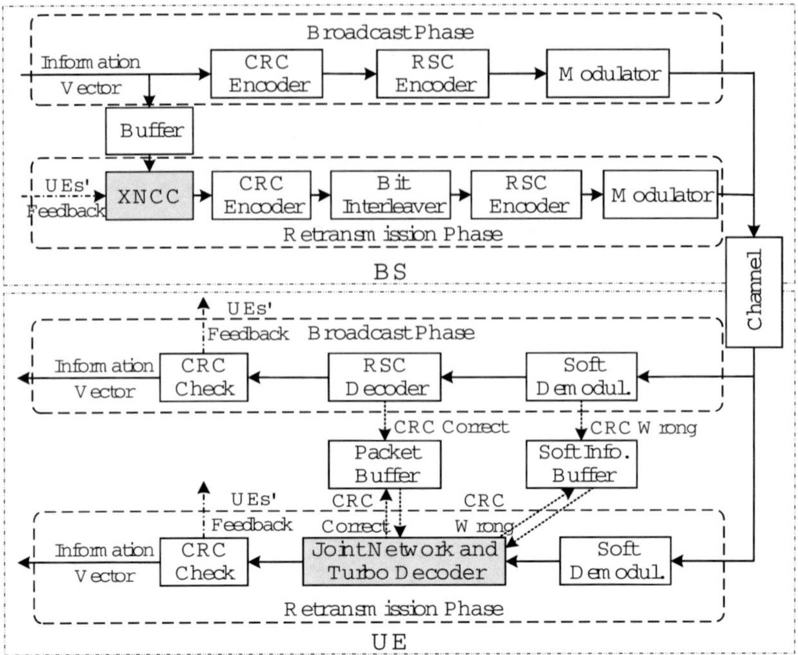

Figure 1. The block diagram of the proposed NTC-HARQ protocol.

- *Œ¨Æ ± – ø ª*: As illustrated in Fig. 1 (BS side), the BS first forms a NC combined retransmission packet by using the proposed XNCC strategy. After passing the CRC encoder, bit interleaver, RSC encoder in sequence, the network coded retransmission packets are broadcasted to UEs by the BS. As illustrated in Fig. 1 (UE side), each UE soft demodulates the received NC combined retransmission packet. Similar to the *◘Æø° ø ¨– ø ª*, each UE sends a HARQ feedback (ACK/NAK) to the BS after JNTD decoding and CRC checking. Specifically, if CRC checking is correct, the correctly received information vector will be stored in the packet buffer. Otherwise, if CRC checking is wrong, the soft information vector will be stored in the soft information buffer.

		Packet ID									
		P_1	P_2	P_3	P_4	P_5	P_6	P_7	P_8	P_9	P_{10}
UE ID	R_1	0	1	1	1	1	0	0	0	0	0
	R_2	0	0	0	0	0	1	1	0	0	1
	R_3	0	0	0	1	0	1	0	0	1	1
	R_4	1	1	1	0	0	0	1	0	0	0
	R_5	0	0	1	0	0	0	0	0	1	1

Figure 2. The example of feedback matrix **T**.

We assume that the BS transmits a WBS frame $\mathcal{X}$, which consisting of λ packets $\mathcal{X} = \{\mathbf{x}_1, \mathbf{x}_2, \cdots, \mathbf{x}_\lambda\}$, in the ■Æø° ø ¨– ø ª. In this paper, an $M \times \lambda$ ªªº æø µ ø¨Æ®**T** is applied to store the state (correctly received or not) of all the packets at each UE. The (i, j)th entry of the matrix **T** $(1 \leq i \leq M, 1 \leq j \leq \lambda)$ indicates whether the ith UE has received packet $\mathbf{x}_j$ or not, i.e., $\mathbf{T}(i, j) = 1$ if $\mathbf{x}_j$ is correctly received by the ith UE, otherwise $\mathbf{T}(i, j) = 0$. The ith column of matrix **T** represents the states whether the ith packet is received successfully or not by all the UEs. The ith row of matrix **T** represents the states whether all the packets are received successfully or not by the ith UE. In other words, rows represent the receiving states of UEs, and columns represent the receiving states of packets.

Different from the traditional NC based type-I HARQ protocol [16, 17, 18, 19, 20, 21, 22], the proposed NTC-HARQ protocol includes a XNCC strategy at the BS and a JNTD strategy at each UE.

3.1. XNCC Strategy

In this paper, the XNCC strategy is proposed to guarantee the efficiency and decodability of the network coded packets. In the Œ¨Æ ± – ø ª, BS forms a ªªº æø µ ø¨Æ®**T** based on UEs' HARQ feedback information, as shown in Fig. 2. When a packet is correctly received by one UE, the corresponding position of the ªªº æø µ ø¨Æ®**T** will be marked as "0", otherwise "1". Hence, matrix **T** can convey two meanings: (1) Whether the packet is lost; (2) The index of UE that lost the packet.

In the proposed XNCC strategy, XORing NC is applied to combine a set of lost packets, which is defined as ø º ºø·ª ª¨. In order to guarantee the efficiency and decodability of the network coded retransmission packets, the ø º ºø·ª ª¨ is generated based on the following two principles: (1) At most one lost packet from each UE is contained in the ø º ºø·ª ª¨, which is to ensure the decodability of the network coded retransmission packet in each UE's network decoder; (2) As many as lost packets of different UEs are contained in the ø º ºø·ª ª¨.

In XNCC strategy, the ø º ºø·ª ª¨ of lost packets is stored in the › ±º Û ¥ ¨and the corresponding UEs' indexes of the lost packets (stored in › ±º Û ¥ ¨) are stored in the À ªÆ ¨. The À ªÆ ¨Ã̱ª is a temporary list. To determine the ø º ºø·ª ª¨ of lost packets, a three steps XNCC strategy based on the ªªº æø µ ø¨Æ®**T** is designed:

- **Step I. Selecting the first packet.** Removing a column in the ªªº Û æø µ ø¨Æ®**T**, where the associated packet of this column is correctly received by all UEs, such as packet ID: 8 in Fig. 2. The packet ID with maximum ºª Æª (number of "1"s in its corresponding column, such as packet ID: 3 in Fig. 2) is stored to › ±º ¥ ¨. The maximum ºª Æª is stored in " ø® ª Æª and the indexes of UEs which lost the corresponding packet are stored in À ªÆ ¨. Removing the corresponding column in the ªªº æø µ ø¨Æ®**T**.

- **Step II. Updating the Codinglist and UserList.** For the ith, $i \in \{1, 2, ..., \lambda\}$, column of matrix **T**, if the ºª Æª of the ith column is equal to " ø® ª Æª, then store the corresponding UE IDs in À ªÆ ¨Ã̱ª. Comparing À ªÆ ¨Ã̱ª with À ªÆ ¨, if there is no intersection, updating À ªÆ ¨ through À ªÆ ¨ $=$ À ªÆ ¨ $\cup$ À ªÆ ¨Ã̱ª, updating › ±º ' ¨through › ±º ¥ ¨ $=$ › ±º ' ¨ $\cup\, i$ and removing the corresponding column in the ªªº æø µ ø¨Æ® **T**. Otherwise, À ªÆ ¨ $=$ À ªÆ ¨ and › ±º ¥ ¨ $=$ › ±º ' ¨. If $(i+1) \leq \lambda$, then empty À ªÆ ¨Ã̱ª and repeat Õª for the $(i+1)$th column of matrix **T**. Otherwise, if $i = \lambda$, then empty À ªÆ ¨Ã̱ª, let " ø® ª Æª$=$" ø® ª Æª-1, $i = 1$, and repeat Õª for the ith column of matrix **T**.

- **Step III. Performing Network Coding.** XORing the packets in › ±º ' ¨ and retransmitting the NC combined packet. If $\sum_{i=1}^{M}\sum_{j=1}^{\lambda}\mathbf{T}(i,j) \neq 0$, then empty › ±º ¥ ¨, À ªÆ ¨ and À ªÆ ¨Ã̱ª and repeat Õª, Õª and Õª. If

$\sum_{i=1}^{M}\sum_{j=1}^{\lambda}\mathbf{T}(i,j)$=0, then the BS updates the feedback matrix **T** and starts the next round of XNCC strategy based on the updated matrix **T**.

According to the above three steps, the XNCC strategy is shown in the **Algorithm 1**, where M denotes the number of UEs, and λ denotes the number of packets.

Example. Applying the proposed XNCC strategy to the feedback matrix **T** given in Fig. 2, we can obtain the combined packets: $P_3 \oplus P_6$, $P_2 \oplus P_{10}$, $P_4 \oplus P_7$, $P_1 \oplus P_5 \oplus P_9$. Under the assumption that the retransmissions are received correctly at all UEs, the number of retransmissions required for the proposed scheme is four, whereas five retransmissions ($P_1 \oplus P_4$, $P_2 \oplus P_6$, $P_3 \oplus P_7$, $P_5 \oplus P_9$, P_{10}) are required for the scheme in [16, 17, 18, 19, 24, 20, 21, 23, 22], and nine retransmissions are required for traditional ARQ.

Since each UE can only recover at most one lost packet during one ŒÛ ¨Æ ± – ø ª, the number of total retransmissions is no less than the maximum number of lost packets among all the UEs. Hence, we note that the minimum number of NC combined packets by using XNCC strategy equals to the maximum number of lost packets among all UEs, which is obvious for the case of two UEs.

3.2. RSC Coding

In the □Æø° ø ¨ – ø ª, the channel code used in the BS is a RSC code with rate R and constraint length K. The feedforward generator is F and the feedback generator is B (both in octal). Due to the systematic nature of the RSC code, the output of the RSC encoder consists of the systematic bits U_b and the parity bits P_b.

In the Œ ¨Æ ± – ø ª, NC combined packet is sent to the CRC encoder and Bit interleaver in sequence, as shown in Fig. 1. Note that a pseudo-random bit interleaver is used in the proposed NTC-HARQ transmission architecture. The interleaved bits are then fed to the RSC encoder. The RSC encoder outputs the systematic bits U_r and the parity bits P_r.

3.3. Joint Network-Turbo Decoding

In the □Æø° ø ¨ – ø ª, each UE can get the soft information of U_b and P_b directly from the received channel codeword. The RSC decoding can

Algorithm 1 The Proposed XNCC strategy

Input: $M \times \lambda$ Feedback Matrix **T**
Export: Combined Packets
  while $\sum_{i=1}^{M}\sum_{j=1}^{\lambda} \mathbf{T}(i,j) \neq 0$ **do**
    sum_per_column = sum(**T**)
    temp = max(sum_per_column)
    for $L = 1$ To λ **do**
      if sum_per_column(L) = temp **then**
        $CodingList = L$
        $UserList = \mathbf{T}(:, L)$
        $\mathbf{T}(:, L) = 0$
        Break
      end if
    end for
    $L = 1$
    if $1 \leq L \leq \lambda$ **then**
      Null À ªÆ ¨·ª
      if sum_per_column(L) = temp **then**
        for $m = 1$ To M **do**
          if **T**(m, L) = 1 **then**
            Update À ªÆ ¨·ª through À ªÆ ¨·ª = À ªÆ ¨·ª $\cup \{m\}$
          end if
        end for
        if À ªÆ ¨·ª ∩À ªÆ ¨ = Null **then**
          Update › ±º ‘ ¨through › ±º ‘ ¨= › ±º ‘ ¨$\cup \{L\}$
          T(:, L) = 0
          Update À ªÆ ¨through À ªÆ ¨= À ªÆ ¨∪ À ªÆ ¨·ª
        end if
        if À ªÆ ¨= all UEs ID **then**
          Break
        end if
      end if
      if $L = \lambda$ **then**
        $L = 1$
        temp = temp-1
      end if
      if temp $= 0$ **then**
        Break
      end if
    end if
    Combined Packets = XOR(› ±º ‘ ¨)
  end while

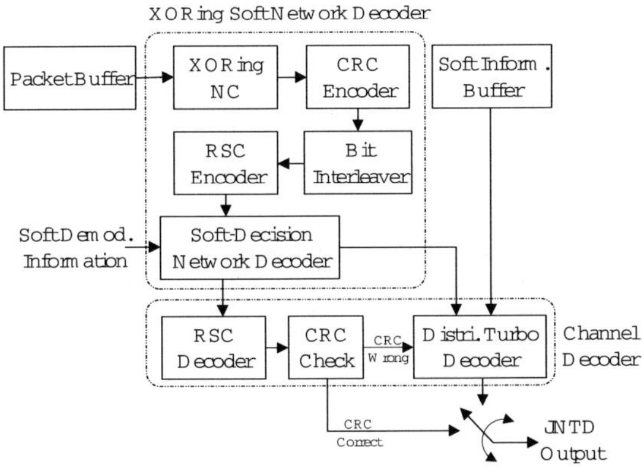

Figure 3. The proposed joint network and turbo decoding architecture.

be done either by soft decision or by hard decision decoder. In addition, the maximum-likelihood method or the MAP principle, namely the viterbi algorithm or the MAP algorithm, can be employed to optimal decode the RSC code.

The proposed JNTD strategy used in the Œ¨Æ ± – ø ª is shown in Fig. 3. After receiving a retransmission packet and the corresponding › ±º Û ' ¨; the lth UE determines whether the received retransmission packet contains their own lost packet. If the desired lost packet of the lth UE is contained in the received NC combined packet, then the lth UE pushes out the corresponding prior successfully received information packets from their packet buffer and XORs them. The combined information packet passes CRC encoder, Bit interleaver and RSC encoder in sequence, which is the same as what has been done in the BS. The output of the RSC encoder $\mathbf{I}_C^l$ is the combination of the packets which are contained in › ±º ' ¨ and successfully received by the lth UE, namely ¥± ø¥ ª ªÆ·ªº ± æ ø¨± ø µª¨.

We assume that the soft-demodulator generates the LLR, namely soft information, for each bit of the combined information packet $\mathbf{C}^l =$ ŒÕ $(\mathbf{I}_L^l \oplus \mathbf{I}_C^l) =$ ŒÕ $(\mathbf{I}_L^l) \oplus$ ŒÕ $(\mathbf{I}_C^l)$, where $\mathbf{I}_L^l$ denotes the information of the lth UE's lost packet. The soft information of the lth UE's lost packet can be obtained by a soft-decision network decoder, which removes the ¥± ø¥ ª ªÆ·ªº ± æ ø¨± ø µª¨ $\mathbf{I}_C^l$ from the soft information of the

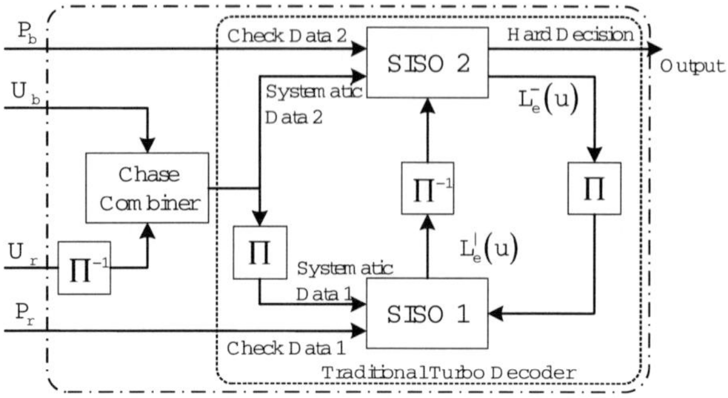

Figure 4. The proposed code combining based distributed turbo decoder.

retransmission packet. Let $\mathbf{C}^l(n)$ and $L[\mathbf{C}^l(n)]$ denote the nth bit of the information $\mathbf{C}^l$ and its LLR value, then the LLR value of $\text{ŒÕ̃}\left(\mathbf{I}_L^l\right)$ can be obtained from (5) by canceling the effect of $\text{ŒÕ̃}\left(\mathbf{I}_C^l\right)$ as:

$$
\begin{aligned}
L[\text{ŒÕ̃}(\mathbf{I}_L^l)](n) &= \log \frac{\Pr\{[\text{ŒÕ̃}(\mathbf{I}_L^l)](n) = 1\}}{\Pr\{[\text{ŒÕ̃}(\mathbf{I}_L^l)](n) = 0\}} \\
&= \begin{cases} L[\mathbf{C}^l](n), \; [\text{ŒÕ̃}(\mathbf{I}_C^l)](n) = 0 \\ -L[\mathbf{C}^l](n), \; [\text{ŒÕ̃}(\mathbf{I}_C^l)](n) = 1 \end{cases}
\end{aligned}
\tag{6}
$$

Hence, by using the soft-decision network decoder, the codewords which are prior known at the UE can be removed before channel decoding, and this operation is transparent to the channel decoder. The soft information of U_r and P_r obtained by using the soft-decision decoder are applied to RSC decoding firstly and then passes the CRC decoder, as shown in Fig. 3. If successful decoding, then the UE get the desired lost packet, otherwise, the soft information of the retransmitted packet (U_r and P_r) and the prior broadcasting packet (U_b and P_b) form a distributed turbo code [31, 32]. By using the proposed chase combining based turbo decoder, the soft information of the retransmitted packet (U_r and P_r) and the prior broadcasting packet (U_b and P_b) can be decoded and the lost packet can be obtained.

Fig. 4 shows the proposed chase combining based distributed turbo decoder, where (Π) denotes the interleaving, and (Π^{-1}) denotes the deinterleaving. Different from the traditional turbo decoder [29], two systematic information streams U_b and $\Pi^{-1}(U_r)$ are chase combined (such as maximum ratio combining), and the combined stream is sent to turbo decoder as the systematic information input. Two MAP based soft-input soft-output (SISO) decoders (SISO1 and SISO2) are used to compute the extrinsic information of the information bit stream, which are represented by $L_e^{|}(u)$ and $L_e^{-}(u)$ in Fig. 4. The extrinsic information is calculated based on the trellis structure of RSC together with the other systematic information and the parity information. We can see from Fig. 4 that the input of SISO1 is the interleaving of systematic information and the retransmitted parity information P_r, and its output information is further de-interleaved to be used as the priori information at the input of SISO2. The input of SISO2 is the systematic information and the parity information P_b of ◘Æ±ø° ø ¨– ø ª, and its output information is then interleaved to be used as the priori information at the input of SISO1 in the next decoding iteration, and can also be used to provide the hard-decision binary final output if needed.

4. Performance Analysis

In this section, the performance of two broadcast protocols (NC based HARQ-I protocol and NC based HARQ-III protocol) are theoretically analyzed. We define the average number of transmissions (ANT) required to successfully broadcast a packet to all the UEs as the metric. In [17], it was shown that the optimal solution of index network coding problem is NP-hard. Hence, a lower bound of ANTs can be obtained through theoretical analyses. Since NC based HARQ-I protocol is based on the typical type-I HARQ technique, the PERs in both ◘Æ±ø° ø ¨– ø ª and Œ¨Æ ± – ø ª are equal. In NC based HARQ-III protocol, by virtue of the code combining, the PER in the Œ¨Æ ± – ø ª is lower than that in the ◘Æ±ø° ø ¨– ø ª. On the other hand, intuitively, the greater the round of retransmissions is, the deeper the fading of lost packets experienced, hence the PER increases as the round of retransmissions increases.

4.1. ANTs Performance of NC Based HARQ-I and NC Based HARQ-III Protocol

In the Œ¨Æ ± – ø ª, at most one lost packet of each UE is contained in the NC combined packet's ø ° °ø·ª ª¨. Meanwhile, if a combined packet is falsely received by a UE, another NC combined packet is needed to ensure this UE is able to obtain the corresponding lost packet. It is implied that the number of NC combined packets is dominated by the UE with largest error probability. Therefore, the total number of transmissions to successfully deliver a NC combined packet to ” UEs is well-approximated to the maximal number of transmissions which is needed to successfully deliver this NC combined packet to the UE with largest error probability.

Suppose that there are ” UEs with PERs P_m, $m \in \{1, \cdots, M\}$, in the ■Æ£ø° ø ¨– ø ª and P^k_{mr}, $m \in \{1, \cdots, M\}$, in the kth Œ¨Æ ± – ø ª. We have the following results:

Proposition 1. The ANTs lower bound of the NC based HARQ-I protocol with ” UEs is

$$\Xi_{N1} = \max_{i=\{1,\cdots M\}} \left\{ \frac{1}{1-P_i} \right\} \tag{7}$$

and the ANTs lower bound of the NC based HARQ-III protocol is

$$\Xi_{N3} = 1 + P_i + \max_{i=\{1,\cdots M\}} \left\{ \sum_{k=2}^{\infty} (k+1) \left(P_i(1-P^k_{ir}) \prod_{j=1}^{k-1} P^j_{ir} \right) - 2P_i P^1_{ir} \right\} \tag{8}$$

Proof. See Appendix A.

4.2. Analysis of Memory Requirement

In this section, the memory requirement of the NC based HARQ protocols is analyzed in detail. Specifically, the retransmission protocols mentioned in this section include: the proposed NTC-HARQ protocol (XNCC+JNTD), NC-HARQ [16, 17, 18, 19, 20, 21, 22] (traditional NC based type-I HARQ), XNCC-HARQ (proposed XNCC based type-I HARQ protocol) and NC[16, 17, 18, 19, 20, 21, 22]-JNTD (traditional NC [16, 17, 18, 19, 20, 21, 22] and proposed JNTD based type-III HARQ protocol).

4.2.1. Memory Requirement at the BS

The memory requirement at the BS for all the protocols is equal to each other. Since all the protocols need to retransmit the lost packets until all the packets within a WBS frame are received correctly by all the UEs. Hence, the memory requirement at the BS is λ packets.

Table 1. Memory Requirements at the UEs.

Protocol	AMR (Packets)	MMR (Packets)
NTC-HARQ	λ	λ
XNCC-HARQ	$(1 - P_e) \times \lambda$	λ
NC[16, 17, 18, 19, 20, 21, 22]-JNTD	λ	λ
NC-HARQ [16, 17, 18, 19, 20, 21, 22]	$(1 - P_e) \times \lambda$	λ

4.2.2. Memory Requirement at the UEs

For the NC based HARQ-I protocols (XNCC-HARQ and NC-HARQ [16, 17, 18, 19, 20, 21, 22]), all the correctly received packets are stored to perform network decoding. Hence, the average memory requirement (AMR) for NC based HARQ-I protocols are $(1 - P_e) \times \lambda$ and the maximum memory requirement (MMR) for NC based HARQ-I protocols are λ, where P_e is the PER in the □Æø° ø ¨– ø ª. For the NC based HARQ-III protocols (NTC-HARQ and NC[16, 17, 18, 19, 20, 21, 22]-JNTD), all the correctly received packets are stored to perform network decoding and all the soft information of the lost packets are stored to perform chase combining. Hence, both the average and maximum memory requirements for NC based HARQ-III protocols are λ. The detailed memory requirements at the UEs are given in Table I.

4.3. Analysis of Computational Complexity

In this section, the computational complexity for all the above mentioned protocols are analyzed in detail. We assume that the number of computations for packet XOR operation is $N_{»–Œ}$ the number of computations for RSC decoder is $N_{ŒÕ}$ and the number of computations for Turbo decoder is $N_{\tilde{A}´Æ}$ Since the computational complexity of the compare operation is small, we omit to calculate this part of complexity.

For the NC based HARQ-I protocols (XNCC-HARQ and NC-HARQ [16, 17, 18, 19, 20, 21, 22]), the number of lost packets is $P_e\lambda$ and the number of packets contained in each NC combined packet is lower bounded as $\frac{\Xi_{“\hat{o}}-1}{P_e\lambda}$. If $\Xi^{»“››}_{“\hat{o}}$ and $\Xi^{“›}_{“\hat{o}}$ denote the ANTs of XNCC-HARQ and NC-HARQ [16, 17, 18, 19, 20, 21, 22] respectively, the number of computations for the

Table 2. Computational Complexity of All the Protocols.

Protocol	Computational Complexity
NTC-HARQ	$\lambda N_{\alpha\tilde{o}} + (\Xi^{\text{»``››}}_{\text{¨}\jmath} - 1)N_{\tilde{A}\text{´Æ}} + (\frac{\Xi^{\text{»``››}}_{\text{¨}\jmath} - 1}{P_e\lambda} - 1)N_{\text{»—Œ}}$
XNCC-HARQ	$\lambda N_{\alpha\tilde{o}} + (\Xi^{\text{»``››}}_{\text{¨}\hat{o}} - 1)N_{\alpha\tilde{o}} + (\frac{\Xi^{\text{»``››}}_{\text{¨}\hat{o}} - 1}{P_e\lambda} - 1)N_{\text{»—Œ}}$
NC[16, 17, 18, 19, 20, 21, 22]-JNTD	$\lambda N_{\alpha\tilde{o}} + (\Xi^{\text{``}}_{\text{¨}\jmath} - 1)N_{\tilde{A}\text{´Æ}} + (\frac{\Xi^{\text{``}}_{\text{¨}\jmath} - 1}{P_e\lambda} - 1)N_{\text{»—Œ}}$
NC-HARQ [16, 17, 18, 19, 20, 21, 22]	$\lambda N_{\alpha\tilde{o}} + (\Xi^{\text{``}}_{\text{¨}\hat{o}} - 1)N_{\alpha\tilde{o}} + (\frac{\Xi^{\text{``}}_{\text{¨}\hat{o}} - 1}{P_e\lambda} - 1)N_{\text{»—Œ}}$

XNCC-HARQ protocol is $\lambda N_{\alpha\tilde{o}} + (\Xi^{\text{»``››}}_{\text{¨}\hat{o}} - 1)N_{\alpha\tilde{o}} + (\frac{\Xi^{\text{»``››}}_{\text{¨}\hat{o}} - 1}{P_e\lambda} - 1)N_{\text{»—Œ}}$ and the number of computations for the NC-HARQ [16, 17, 18, 19, 20, 21, 22] protocol is $\lambda N_{\alpha\tilde{o}} + (\Xi^{\text{``}}_{\text{¨}\hat{o}} - 1)N_{\alpha\tilde{o}} + (\frac{\Xi^{\text{``}}_{\text{¨}\hat{o}} - 1}{P_e\lambda} - 1)N_{\text{»—Œ}}$

For the NC based HARQ-III protocols (NTC-HARQ and NC[16, 17, 18, 19, 20, 21, 22]-JNTD), the number of lost packets is $P_e\lambda$ and the number of packets contained in each NC combined packet is lower bounded as $\frac{\Xi_{\text{¨}\jmath} - 1}{P_e\lambda}$. If $\Xi^{\text{»``››}}_{\text{¨}\jmath}$ and $\Xi^{\text{``}}_{\text{¨}\jmath}$ denote the ANTs of NTC-HARQ and NC[16, 17, 18, 19, 20, 21, 22]-JNTD respectively, the number of computations for the NTC-HARQ protocol is $\lambda N_{\alpha\tilde{o}} + (\Xi^{\text{»``››}}_{\text{¨}\jmath} - 1)N_{\tilde{A}\text{´Æ}} + (\frac{\Xi^{\text{»``››}}_{\text{¨}\jmath} - 1}{P_e\lambda} - 1)N_{\text{»—Œ}}$and the number of computations for the NC[16, 17, 18, 19, 20, 21, 22]-JNTD protocol is $\lambda N_{\alpha\tilde{o}} + (\Xi^{\text{``}}_{\text{¨}\jmath} - 1)N_{\tilde{A}\text{´Æ}} + (\frac{\Xi^{\text{``}}_{\text{¨}\jmath} - 1}{P_e\lambda} - 1)N_{\text{»—Œ}}$

As shown in the next chapter, the ANTs performances of the proposed XNCC based protocols (NTC-HARQ and XNCC-HARQ protocol) outperform that of the traditional NC [16, 17, 18, 19, 20, 21, 22] based corresponding protocols (NC[16, 17, 18, 19, 20, 21, 22]-JNTD and NC-HARQ [16, 17, 18, 19, 20, 21, 22] protocol), respectively. Hence the computational complexity of the proposed NTC-HARQ protocol is lower than NC[16, 17, 18, 19, 20, 21, 22]-JNTD protocol and XNCC-HARQ protocol is lower than NC-HARQ [16, 17, 18, 19, 20, 21, 22] protocol. The detailed computational complexity is shown in Table II.

5. Simulation Results

In this section, we carry out numerical simulations to testify the performance of the proposed XNCC and JNTD based HARQ protocols. Consider a wireless broadcasting scenario where a BS wants to transmit a frame of λ packets

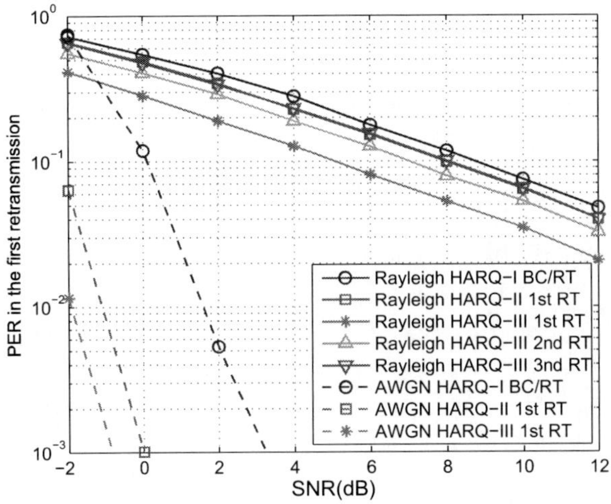

Figure 5. The PER performances of three HARQ protocols over AWGN and Rayleigh block fading channel.

to M UEs. We assume that the channels between BS and UEs subject to same complex Gaussian distribution $\mathcal{CN}\left(0, \sigma_h^2\right)$ with $\sigma_h^2 = 1$ and BS's transmission power P_s is normalized. SNR used in this chapter is the ratio between transmit power and noise power (i.e., transmit SNR). The channel code used in this chapter is a rate R=1/2 RSC code with constraint length K=5. The feedforward generator is F=37 and the feedback generator is B=21 (both in octal). The length of information packet is L = 200 bits (containing CRC bits), and the length of coded packet is L, =400 bits. It is assumed that 8 iterations are performed in turbo decoder. We consider simulation results for the proposed three protocols: NTC-HARQ protocol (XNCC+JNTD), XNCC-HARQ protocol (XNCC+Type-I HARQ) and NC[16, 17, 18, 19, 20, 21, 22]-JNTD protocol (traditional NC[16, 17, 18, 19, 20, 21, 22]+JNTD), and compare the proposed three protocols with the reference protocol (the index NC [16, 17, 18, 19, 20, 21, 22] based NC-HARQ protocol).

The PER performances of three types of HARQ protocols are shown in Fig. 5. We can see from Fig. 5 that the PER performance of the type-III HARQ protocol over AWGN channel outperforms that of the type-II HARQ protocol about 1dB. Thanks to the maximum ratio combining, the PER performance of the type-II HARQ outperforms that of the type-I HARQ about 3dB. Comparing with type-I HARQ, the performance gain of type-II HARQ in the first ŒˆÆ ± – ø ª over Rayleigh block fading channel is less than 1dB although chase combining is employed. This is because, in the first ŒˆÆ ± – ø ª of type-II HARQ, the chase combining is only performed on the incorrect packet and the retransmission packet, and the incorrect packet is subject to severe fading, hence, only a small diversity gain can be obtained by the retransmission packet due to chase combining. The performance gap between type-III HARQ protocol and type-I HARQ protocol in the first ŒˆÆ ± – ø ª is about 3.5dB, which is less than the performance gap between turbo code and RSC. This is because, in the first ŒˆÆ ± – ø ª of type-III HARQ, the incorrect packet and the retransmission packet form a distributed turbo code to obtain the code combining gain. Different from traditional turbo code, which is built on two identical RSC codes and subject to the same fading, the undecodable RSC partition of distributed turbo code is subject to deep fading. Hence, the total gain will not be very large compared with traditional turbo code. Meanwhile, intuitively, the greater the round of retransmissions is, the deeper the fading of lost packets experienced, hence the PER increases with the increasing of the round of retransmissions as it is can be seen from Fig. 5.

Fig. 6 shows the simulation results of the average number of lost packets included in each network coded packet (ANLPinNC) as a function of Signal-to-Noise-Rate (SNR), where ANLPinNC can be given by the equation $N_{\square\cdots\_\ \cdots} = P_L/N_{\cdots}$, P_L denotes the total number of lost packets needed to be retransmitted and $N_{\cdots}$ denotes the number of the network coded packets. The number of packets within a frame is $\lambda = 100$. We can see from Fig. 6 that the proposed XNCC strategy outperforms traditional index NC [16, 17, 18, 19, 20, 21, 22] scheme. At low SNR, each UE lost a large number of packets, which leads to a low probability of successfully combining a NC packet, hence the ANLPinNC performance gain approaches to zero. At high SNR, the PER at each UE is low and the ªªº æø µ øˆÆ®T is with low density, which results in an approaching to 1 maximum ºª Æª, hence the ANLPinNC performance of traditional index NC [16, 17, 18, 19, 20, 21, 22] scheme approaches to that of the proposed XNCC strategy.

The ANLPinNC performances of the proposed XNCC strategy versus traditional index NC [16, 17, 18, 19, 20, 21, 22] scheme at SNR = 4dB are demonstrated in Fig. 7. We can see from Fig. 7 that the proposed XNCC

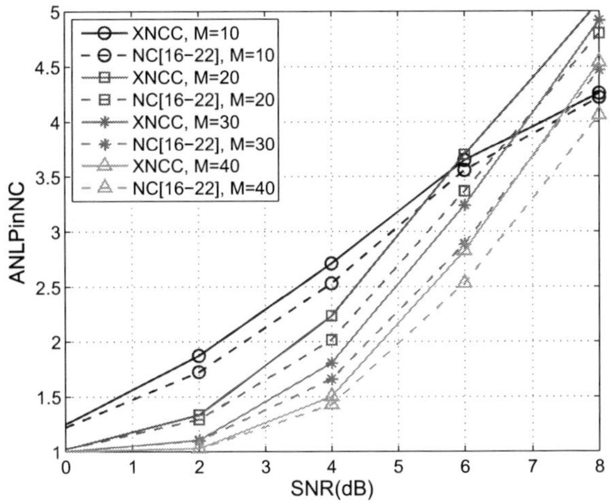

Figure 6. Average number of lost packets included in each network coded packet versus SNR, $\lambda = 100$.

strategy outperforms traditional index NC [16, 17, 18, 19, 20, 21, 22] scheme on the ANLPinNC performance, and the ANLPinNC performance increases as λ increases.

Fig. 8 demonstrates the ANLPinNC performances of NTC-HARQ versus NC[16, 17, 18, 19, 20, 21, 22]-JNTD as the round of retransmissions increases at SNR=-2dB. The number of packets within a frame is $\lambda = 100$. We can see from Fig. 8 that the proposed NTC-HARQ protocol outperforms NC[16, 17, 18, 19, 20, 21, 22]-JNTD protocol on the ANLPinNC performance. Hence, we can conclude from Fig. 8 that the proposed XNCC strategy outperforms traditional index NC [16, 17, 18, 19, 20, 21, 22] on the reduction of retransmissions. Moreover, we can see from Fig. 8 that the ANLPinNC performance of NTC-HARQ equals to NC[16, 17, 18, 19, 20, 21, 22]-JNTD in the first round of retransmission. This is because the probability of all the lost packets to form a NC combined packet approaches to zero in the first round of retransmission at SNR=-2dB and almost all the retransmission packets are single lost packets (without NC combined).

Fig. 9 shows the simulation results of ANTs versus SNR to validate the performance of the proposed JNTD strategy. The number of packets within

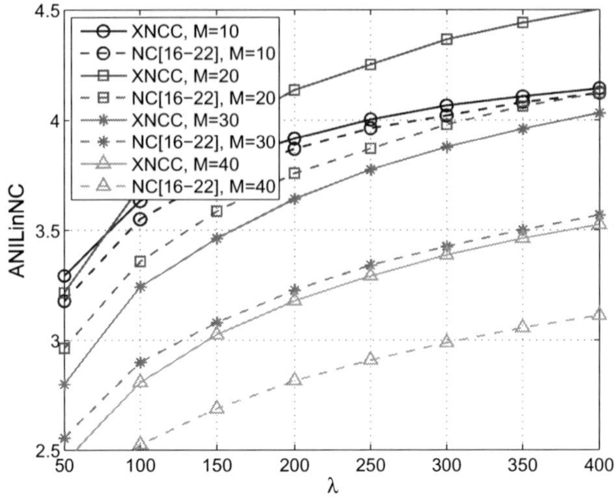

Figure 7. Average number of lost packets included in each network coded packet versus λ, SNR= 4dB.

a frame is $\lambda = 100$. The numerical results of the theoretical analyses in (7) and (8) are also depicted for comparison. We can see from Fig. 9 that the exact ANTs performances of the proposed NTC-HARQ protocol and XNCC-HARQ protocol derived by Monte Carlo simulations for M=2 match well with the theoretical analyses in (7) and (8), respectively. Meanwhile, simulation results show that the proposed JNTD based HARQ protocol (NTC-HARQ protocol) achieves a significant ANTs performance gain when compared with the type-I HARQ based protocol (XNCC-HARQ protocol), even though the proposed XNCC strategy is applied in the XNCC-HARQ protocol.

Fig. 10 simulates the ANTs performances as a function of SNR for 10 and 30 UEs. The number of packets within a frame is $\lambda = 100$. We can see from Fig. 10 that there is a sharp ANTs decrease when compare the proposed XNCC and JNTD based retransmission protocol (NTC-HARQ) with the traditional index NC [16, 17, 18, 19, 20, 21, 22] based retransmission protocol (NC-HARQ [16, 17, 18, 19, 20, 21, 22]). The proposed NTC-HARQ protocol (XNCC+JNTD) outperforms XNCC-JNTD-Sel protocol (XNCC+JNTD with Selective Combining), NC[16, 17, 18, 19, 20, 21, 22]-JNTD protocol

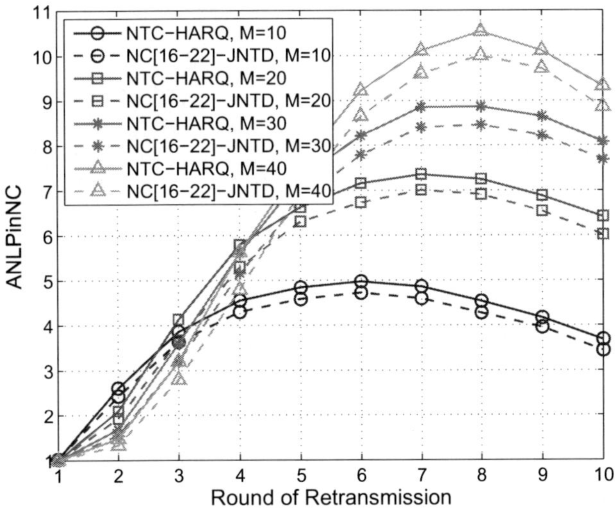

Figure 8. Average number of lost packets included in each network coded packet versus round of retransmissions. SNR=-2dB, $\lambda = 100$.

(traditional NC[16, 17, 18, 19, 20, 21, 22]+JNTD). Meanwhile, it can be seen from Fig. 10 that there is an ANTs performance gap between the proposed NTC-HARQ protocol and the lower bound (8) when M=10, 30. This is because the optimal solution of index network coding problem is NP-hard [17], even through the proposed XNCC strategy outperforms traditional index network coding scheme [16, 17, 18, 19, 20, 21, 22], but it is not yet the optimal solution.

Fig. 11 shows the simulation results of ANTs performances as a function of λ for M=10 and 30 UEs. The SNR is fixed at SNR=0dB. We can see from Fig. 11 that the proposed XNCC based HARQ protocols (NTC-HARQ, XNCC-JNTD-Sel) outperform traditional NC [16, 17, 18, 19, 20, 21, 22] based HARQ protocols (NC[16, 17, 18, 19, 20, 21, 22]-JNTD, NC-HARQ [16, 17, 18, 19, 20, 21, 22]) on the ANTs performance. Meanwhile, ANTs performance floor can be observed in the large λ region for all the protocols, which suggests the inherent performance gap between the proposed XNCC strategy and the optimal index network coding solution.

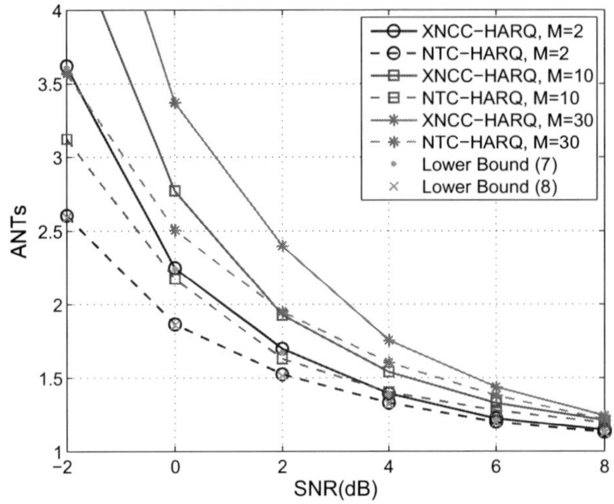

Figure 9. Average number of transmissions versus SNR. $\lambda = 100$ and $L_{,} = 400$.

Fig. 12 demonstrates the ANTs performances of each protocol as the number of UEs increases for a fixed number of packets $\lambda = 100$. The SNR is fixed at SNR= 0dB. As shown in the figure, there is a sharp ANTs decrease when applying the proposed JNTD schemes to the NC (XNCC and traditional NC) based data broadcasting protocols. Meanwhile, the ANTs increases as the number of UEs M increases for all the protocols. The proposed NTC-HARQ protocol obtains the best ANTs performance when compared with other protocols.

6. Conclusion

In this paper, a network coding and distributed turbo coding based type-III HARQ protocol, named as NTC-HARQ protocol, is proposed to increase the bandwidth efficiency of wireless broadcasting systems. The main idea is to retransmit packets of many users simultaneously using NC and recover the soft information of lost packets by performing joint network and turbo decoding in Œ¨Æ ± − ∅ ª. The advantages of the proposed schemes over the traditional retransmission schemes are shown through theoretical analy-

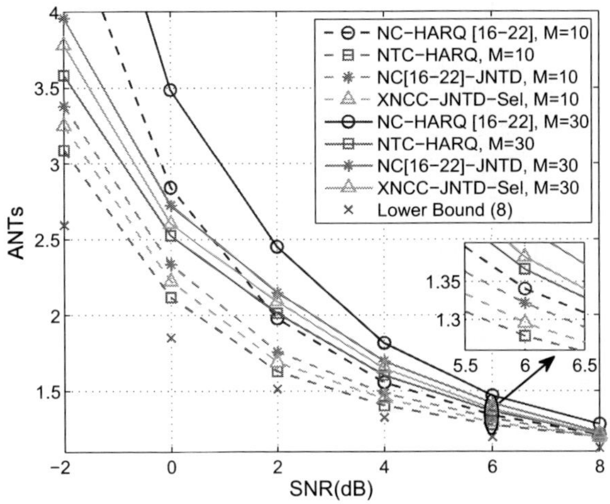

Figure 10. Average number of transmissions versus SNR. $M = 10$, $\lambda = 100$ and $L_{,} = 400$.

ses and simulations. Comparing with NC-HARQ protocol, XNCC-HARQ protocol and NC-JNTD protocol, NTC-HARQ protocol can significantly reduce the number of transmissions per successful packet, whose gains is attributed to the potential advantage of XNCC strategy and the better PER performance of JNTD strategy.

Appendix A

A. Proof of Proposition 1

For the NC based HARQ-III protocol, the number of transmissions needed to successfully deliver a packet to an UE with the PERs P_i and P_{ir}^k, $k \geq 1$, is a random variable «. We have

$$P[Y = 1] = 1 - P_i \tag{9}$$

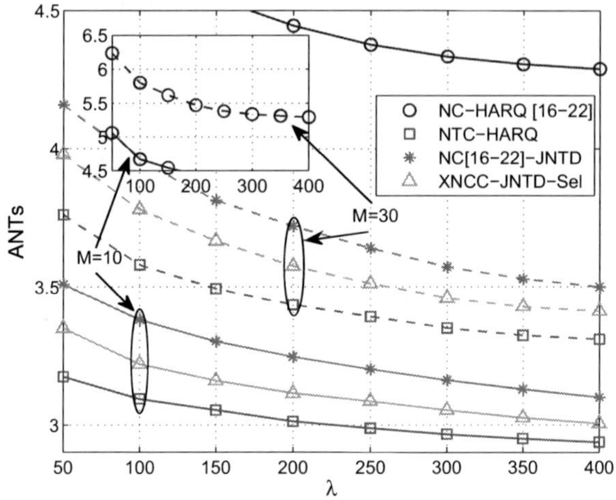

Figure 11. Average number of transmissions versus λ. $M = 10$ and SNR=-2dB.

and

$$\begin{aligned} P[Y \leq k+1] &= 1 - P[Y > k+1] \\ &= 1 - P_i \prod_{j=1}^{k} P_{ir}^{j} \quad (k \geq 1) \end{aligned} \tag{10}$$

Therefore,

$$P[Y = 2] = P_i(1 - P_{ir}^{1}) \tag{11}$$

and

$$\begin{aligned} P[Y = k+1] &= \left(1 - P_i \prod_{j=1}^{k} P_{ir}^{j}\right) - \left(1 - P_i \prod_{j=1}^{k-1} P_{ir}^{j}\right) \\ &= P_i \prod_{j=1}^{k-1} P_{ir}^{j} - P_i \prod_{j=1}^{k} P_{ir}^{j} \\ &= P_i(1 - P_{ir}^{k}) \prod_{j=1}^{k-1} P_{ir}^{j} \quad (k \geq 2) \end{aligned} \tag{12}$$

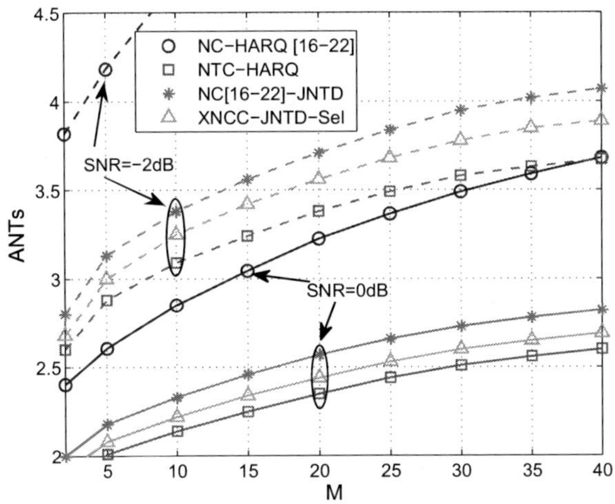

Figure 12. Average number of transmissions versus M, $\lambda = 100$.

and the ANTs per successful packet is

$$\begin{aligned} E[Y] &= \sum_{k=1}^{\infty} kP[Y=k] \\ &= 1 + P_i - 2P_iP_{ir}^1 + \sum_{k=2}^{\infty}(k+1)\left(P_i(1-P_{ir}^k)\prod_{j=1}^{k-1}P_{ir}^j\right) \end{aligned} \tag{13}$$

Thus the ANTs of NC based HARQ-III protocol with M UEs is

$$\begin{aligned} \Xi_{N3} &= \max_{i=\{1,\cdots M\}}\{E[Y]\} \\ &= 1 + P_i + \max_{i=\{1,\cdots M\}}\left\{\sum_{k=2}^{\infty}(k+1)\left(P_i(1-P_{ir}^k)\prod_{j=1}^{k-1}P_{ir}^j\right) - 2P_iP_{ir}^1\right\} \end{aligned} \tag{14}$$

For NC based HARQ-I protocol, let $P_i = P_{ir}^k$, We have

$$\begin{aligned} \Xi_{N1} &= 1 + \max_{i=\{1,\cdots M\}}\left\{\frac{P_i}{1-P_i}\right\} \\ &= \max_{i=\{1,\cdots M\}}\left\{\frac{1}{1-P_i}\right\} \end{aligned} \tag{15}$$

References

[1] J.-F. Cheng, "Coding performance of hybrid ARQ schemes," ¤¤¤ ÃÆƃ Ú ± ´ ø¨± , vol. 54, no. 6, pp. 1017-1029, Jun. 2006.

[2] Y. Wang, L. Zhang, and D. Yang, "Performance analysis of type III HARQ with turbo codes," in –Æ± Ú¤¤¤ Ã› Ó Ì , vol. 4, pp. 2740-2744, Apr. 2003.

[3] R. Bosisio, U. Spagnolini, and Y. Bar-Ness, "Multilevel Type-II HARQ with Adaptive Modulation Control," in –Æ± Ú ¤¤¤ …› "› Ó Í , vol. 4, pp. 2082-2087, Apr. 2006.

[4] X. Xia, Y. Xu, K. Xu, D. Zhang, N. Li, "Outage performance of AF-based time division broadcasting protocol in the presence of co-channel interference," in –Æ± ÚÓ Ộ ¤¤¤ … Æ¥ › ± ´ ø¨± ø º "ª¨©±Æ ›± ªÆ ª ¯…› "› ˜, pp. 3482-3487, 7-10 April 2013.

[5] Y. Xu, X. Xia, K. Xu, Y. Chen, "Symbol error rate of two-way decode-and-forward relaying with co-channel interference," in –Æ± ÚÓ Ộ ¤¤¤ Ộ¨ ¨ªÆø¨± ø¥Õß ± ´ ± –ªÆ± ø¥ º±±Æø º " ±æ¥ Œø º ±› ± ´ ø¨± ¯ " Œ ˜, pp. 138-143, 8-11 Sept. 2013.

[6] K. Xu, D. Zhang, Y. Xu, W. Ma, "On the Equivalence of Two Optimal Power-Allocation Schemes for A-TWRC," ¤¤¤ ÃÆƃ ø ¨± ± ª ´¥øÆÃª ±¥± ß, vol. 63, no. 4, pp. 1970-1976, May 2014.

[7] R. Ahlswede, N. Cai, S-Y.R. Li, and R.W. Yeung, "Network Information Flow," ¤¤¤ ÃÆƃ Ú ±Æ ø¨± Ã ª±ÆßB, vol. 46, no. 4, pp. 1204-1216, Jul. 2000.

[8] X. Xia, D. Zhang, K. Xu, Y. Xu, "Interference-Limited Two-Way DF Relaying: Symbol-Error-Rate Analysis and Comparison," ¤¤¤ ÃÆƃ ø ¨± ± ª ´¥øÆÃª ±¥± ß, vol. 63, no. 7, pp. 3474-3480, Sept. 2014.

[9] Z. Ding, Z. Ma, and K.K. Leung, "Impact of Network Coding on System Delay for Multisource-Multidestination Scenarios," ¤¤¤ ÃÆƃ Û ø ¨± ± ª ´¥øÆÃª ±¥± ß, vol. 59, no. 2, pp. 831-841, Feb. 2010.

[10] X. Xia, K. Xu, W. Ma, Y. Xu, "On the design of relay selection strategy for two-way amplify-and-forward mobile relaying," ¤Ã › ± ´Û ø¨± , vol. 7, no. 17, pp. 1948-1957, Nov. 26 2013.

[11] Chiti F., Fantacci R., Tassi A., "An Efficient Network Coding Scheme With Symbol Combining: Performance Evaluation, Optimization, and Comparisons," ¤¤¤ ÃÆ ø ¨± ± ª ´¥ÆÃª ±¥ ß, vol. 62, no. 3, pp. 1267-1275, Mar. 2013.

[12] E. Ahmed, A. Eryilmaz, M. Medard, and A. Ozdaglar, "On the Scaling Law of Network Coding Gains in Wireless Networks," in –Æ Ú¤¤¤ " ' › —" Ó È, pp. 1-7, Oct. 2007.

[13] T. Ho, R. Koetter, M. Medard, D.R. Karger, and M. Effros, "The benefits of coding over routing in a randomized setting," in –Æ Ú¤¤¤ ·ªÆø¨± ø¥Ãß ± ´ ± ±Æ ÚÃ ª±ß Ó Ì , pp. 442, July 2003.

[14] Hongkun Xi, Xiaoxiang Wang, Yuan Zhao, Hongtao Zhang, "A Reliable Broadcast Transmission Approach Based on Random Linear Network Coding," in –Æ Ú¤¤¤ ÈÎ¨ ª ´¥ÆÃª ±¥ ß › ± ªÆ ª ¯ Ã› Õ Æ ˜Ó ÔÓ, pp. 1-5, May 2012.

[15] A. Eryilmaz, A. Ozdaglar, M. Medard, Ebad Ahmed, "On the Delay and Throughput Gains of Coding in Unreliable Networks," in ¤¤¤ ÃÆ ø ¨± ± ±Æ ø¨± Ã ª±ß, vol. 54, no. 12, pp. 5511-5524, Dec. 2008.

[16] M. A. R. Chaudhry and A. Sprintson, "Efficient algorithms for index coding," in –Æ Ú¤¤¤ "□—› —" …±ß ± Ó Ë, pp. 1-4, 2008.

[17] Z. Bar-Yossef, Y. Birk, T. Jayram, and T. Kol, "Index coding with side information," ¤¤¤ ÃÆ ø ¨± ± ±Æ ø¨± Ã ª±ß, vol. 57, pp. 1479-1494, 2011.

[18] S.K. Hong, and J.-M. Chung, "Network-coding-based hybrid ARQ scheme for mobile relay networks," ¤Ã ¤¥ ¨Æ ' ª··ª Æ, vol. 46, no. 7, pp. 539-541, Apr. 2010.

[19] Lu Lu, Ming Xiao, Skoglund M., Rasmussen L., Gang Wu, Shaoqian Li, "Efficient Network Coding for Wireless Broadcasting," in –Æ Ú

¤¤¤ … Æ¥ª › ± ´ ø¨ ± ø º “ª ¨©±Æ › ± ªÆ ª ¯…› “› ˜ Ó Ô , pp. 1-6, Apr. 2010.

[20] Sorour S., Valaee S., “An Adaptive Network Coded Retransmission Scheme for Single-Hop Wireless Multicast Broadcast Services,” ¤¤¤ › ” ÃÆ ø ¨± ± “ª ¨©±Æ , vol. 19, no. 3, pp. 869-878, Jun. 2011.

[21] Fei Wu, Cunqing Hua, Hangguan Shan, Aiping Huang, “Reliable network coding for minimizing decoding delay and feedback overhead in wireless broadcasting,” in –Æ Ú¤¤¤ Ô Æ ¨ªÆø¨± ø¥Õß ± ´ ± –ªÆ± ø¥ º±±Æø º ” ±æ¥ Œø º ± › ± ´ ø¨ ± ¯ – ” Œ ˜ Ó ÔÓ, pp. 796-801, Sep. 2012.

[22] D. Nguyen, T. Tran, T. Nguyen, and B. Bose, “Wireless broadcast using network coding,” ¤¤¤ ÃÆ Ú ª ´¥øÆÃª ±¥± ß, vol. 58, no. 2, pp. 914-925, Feb. 2009.

[23] J. Li, Z. Hu, Y. Wang, “Compressed Multicast Retransmission in LTE-A eMBMS,” in –Æ Ú¤¤¤ ÈÔ ¨ ª ´¥øÆÃª ±¥± ß › ± ªÆ ª ¯ Ã› Ó Ô ÛÕ Æ ˜Ó Ô , pp. 1-4, May 2010.

[24] Zhang Zhang, Tiejun Lv, Xin Su, Hui Gao, “Dual XOR in the Air: A Network Coding Based Retransmission Scheme for Wireless Broadcasting,” in –Æ Ú¤¤¤ ¨ªÆø¨± ø¥› ± ªÆ ª ± › ± ´ ø¨ ± ¯› › ˜Ó ÔÔ, pp. 1-6, Jun. 2011.

[25] Manssour J., Osseiran A., Slimane S.B., “A Unicast Retransmission Scheme Based on Network Coding,” ¤¤¤ ÃÆ ø ¨± ± ª ´¥øÆ Ãª ±¥± ß, vol. 61, no. 2, pp. 871-876, Feb. 2012.

[26] Thobaben, Ragnar, “Joint Network/Channel Coding for Multi-User Hybrid-ARQ,” in –Æ ÚÈ¨ ¨ªÆø¨± ø¥ ÃŸ › ± ªÆ ª ± Õ±´Æª ø º › ø ª¥› ±º ¯Õ › ˜Ó Ë, pp. 1-6, 14-16 Jan. 2008.

[27] Yidong Lang, Wubben D., Dekorsy A., Braun V., Doetsch U., “Improved HARQ based on network coding and its application in LTE,” in –Æ Ú¤¤¤ … Æ¥ª › ± ´ ø¨ ± ø º “ª ¨©±Æ › ± ªÆ ª ¯…› “› ˜Ó ÔÓ, pp. 1958-1963, Apr. 2012.

[28] Zheng Guo, Jie Huang, Bing Wang, Shengli Zhou, Jun-Hong Cui, Willett P., "A Practical Joint Network-Channel Coding Scheme for Reliable Communication in Wireless Networks," ¤¤¤ ÃÆ ø ¨± ± …Æ¥ › ± ´ ø¨± , vol. 11, no. 6, pp. 2084-2094, June 2012.

[29] D. Divsalar, S. Dolinar, F. Pollara, "Iterative turbo decoder analysis based on density evolution," ¤¤¤ ÷±´Æø¥± Õ¥ ·ªº ▫Æø › ± Û ´ ø¨± , vol. 19, no. 5, pp. 891-907, May 2001.

[30] J. Hagenauer, › ± ´ ø¨± Ù ±º ø º › Æß Æ¥± ß, Springer, pp. 155-171, 1994.

[31] Yonghui Li, B. Vucetic, T.F. Wong, M. Dohler, "Distributed Turbo Coding With Soft Information Relaying in Multihop Relay Networks," ¤¤¤ ÷±´Æø¥± Õ¥ ·ªº ▫Æø › ± ´ ø¨± , vol. 24, no. 11, pp. 2040-2050, Nov. 2006.

[32] L. Maret, D. Ktenas, "Distributed Turbo Coding Techniques with HARQ at Relays for LTE-A," in –Æ Ú¤¤¤ ÈÈ¨ ª ´¥øÆÃª ±¥Û ± ß› ± ªÆ ª ¯ Ã› Õ Æ ˜Ó Ô , pp. 1-5, 2-5 June 2013.

[33] Biglieri Ezio, › ±º ±Æ.. Æ¥ › ø ª¥ , Springer, 2005.

[34] H. Shin, S. Kim, J. H. Lee, Turbo decoding in a Rayleigh fading channel with estimated channel state information, ª ´¥øÆÃª ±¥± ß › ± ªÆ ª, 2000. IEEE-VTS Fall VTC 2000. 52nd, vol. 3, pp. 1358-1363, 2000.

In: Network Coding and Data Compression ISBN: 978-1-63483-185-7
Editor: MaryAnn Simmons © 2015 Nova Science Publishers, Inc.

Chapter 4

MINIMUM ENERGY MULTICAST IN WIRELESS NETWORKS: EMPIRICAL STUDY OF CODED PACKET MODEL

Adeyemi Abel Ajibesin[1,2,*] and Neco Ventura[1]
[1]Department of Electrical Engineering, University of Cape Town, Cape Town, Western Cape, South Africa
[2]School of Information Technology & Computing, American University of Nigeria, Nigeria

Abstract

In routing, the problem of performing minimum energy multicast considering Wireless Multicast Advantage (WMA) is difficult. This is because, the problem of minimum energy broadcast that is solved easily in the wire line case by various minimum weights panning tree algorithms, becomes NP-complete. However, alternative approach using heuristics method is employed. An example of this method is the Multicast Incremental Power (MIP) algorithm. The coding technique has further simplified the problem of minimum energy multicast. This is achieved by solving the problem of minimum energy multicast in polynomial time. As a result, optimal energy is less when coding is used compared to routing technique. Hence, coding in packet networks (network coding) is a promising approach

* E-mail address: ajibesin@ieee.org; Address: Electrical Engineering Department, University of Cape Town, Rondebosch 7001, Cape Town, Western Cape, South Africa (Corresponding author).

for minimum energy multicast. Simulation results have shown that coding can reduce between 13% to 49% average total multicast energy in random wireless networks of varying size over MIP technique. Therefore, in terms of reducing the multicast energy, coded packet technique outperformed the MIP technique. Furthermore, it was observed that polynomial-time solution is not enough to address the problem of minimum energy multicast. This is because the solution was based on centralised computation, which is not suitable for many applications. As a result, a decentralized solution was proposed for optimisation in network coding. However, there is a need to further reduce the multicast energy in coded packet networks using appropriate model. This study reveals that though various solutions were proposed for minimum energy multicast but, they did not address the efficiency of the networks adequately. This rendered both the centralized and decentralised coding techniques inefficient. This chapter seeks to answer the questions: How a network performance could be evaluated against the best-practice frontier networks? How could expected minimum energy in wireless network be achieved? These questions are addressed by studying the minimum energy multicast over coded packet networks and proposed alternative method based on empirical Data Envelopment Analysis (DEA) methodology. The study shows that substantial amount of energy could be reduced if the right model is used and the networks operate efficiently. The results are then analysed and compared with the current techniques.

1. Introduction

The main optimization problem for energy efficiency broadcast/multicast routing in wireless networks is to minimize the total transmission power assigned to all nodes [1]. This is widely recognized as one of the most performance challenges in wireless networking technologies. The minimum energy multicast problem in wireless networks is solvable as a linear programming, assuming coded packet technique [2]. Comparing this technique with conventional routing solutions, coded packet technique not only promises a potentially lower multicast energy, but also enables finding the optimal solution in polynomial time, in sharp contrast with the NP-hardness of constructing the minimum energy multicast tree as the optimal routing solution. In this chapter, the minimum energy multicast framework involving coding is considered and extended so as to further minimize multicast energy in wireless networks. Other recent energy efficiency frameworks that were presented in the literature include virtualization technique for energy reduction in data centers [3], [4]. However, they were all designed to achieve similar goal using effective performance evaluation approach [1], [5]. This work adopts a ratio efficiency approach to energy optimization problem and then presents an empirical DEA architecture for energy efficiency in multicast wireless networks.

To address the energy efficiency challenges, this chapter presents three models that are based on Data Envelopment Analysis (DEA) methodology to appropriately evaluate the efficiency of multicast energy and further minimises energy transmission in wireless networks without affecting the overall network performance. The DEA, which was used to study the relative efficiency and productivity of systems in Economic and Operational Research (OR) disciplines, is a non-parametric method that relies on linear programming technique for optimisation of discrete units of observation called the Decision Making Units (DMUs) [6]. Thus, the main goal of this work was to design an empirical DEA architecture that incorporates envelopment model for technical efficiency measure, slack model for energy projection and energy gap (EG) for estimating the amount of energy saved. Furthermore, the model formulation adopted the Charnes, Cooper and Rhodes (CCR) basic model to achieve input-oriented CCR with the assumption of constant returns to scale (CRS) in comparison with the existing techniques in literature for the implementation of envelopment model in wireless networks. Subsequently, the Slack model was formulated to improve the performance of the envelopment model. Then the gap analysis is performed to evaluate the energy saved.

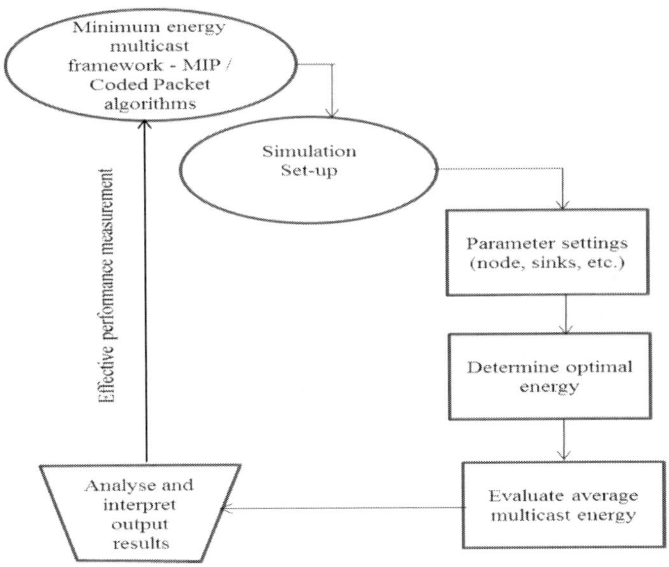

Figure 1.1. Block Diagram of Minimum Energy Multicast.

The remainder of this chapter is presented in sections: section 2 provides necessary background information on the minimum energy multicast framework, section 3 presents the empirical DEA architecture and derived the models for minimum energy multicast networks. In section 4, the empirical DEA results are analyzed and discussed, section 5 presents the amount of energy saved if the proposed model is considered while section 6 summarily concludes the chapter.

2. Minimum Energy Multicast Framework

Figure 1.1 summarizes the minimum energy multicast model, which include models for the MIP and coded packet algorithms with the focus on the later. The coded packet technique and its algorithm are further explained in section 2.1 and 2.2 respectively. The framework defines the performance metric and simulation parameters in section 2.3 while section 2.4 presented the simulation results. Observe from Figure 1, that the simulation is setup according to the coded packet algorithm requirements and the inputs parameters such as node and sinks are configured. The algorithm is run based on these parameters (node, sinks, etc.) set for each wireless network scenario and the optimal value of the multicast energy for each of these networks are obtained. Then, the average of these values is evaluated using a statistical mean and standard deviation.

2.1. Coded Packet Technique and Assumptions

In literature, the MIP technique adopted WMA to minimise multicast energy but this heuristics approach to reduce multicast energy is sub-optimal. In order to achieve improved minimum energy multicast, coding technique was introduced. The coding technique considered optimisation of minimum energy multicast using linear programming. In coding, optimal energy is expected to be less when compared to MIP technique. The coding employed a flow-based approach for addressing networks with costs (e.g., energy) using linear programming framework [2], [7]. This cost is a function of coding subgraph z. Considering a situation whereby ξ represents the cost function and assumed that ξ is convex. Flow-based approach assumes that all nodes in the network are capable of coding, and focus on the problem of minimizing resources (e.g., energy) that can be expressed as a function of the coding subgraph z. As it relates to this study, energy is considered as the main resource to be minimised. Again, the energy is denoted with ξ function, then the formulation of a multicast problem connection is considered to be a triplet $\left(S,T,\{R_t\}\right)_{t\in T}$, where S is the source of the connection, T is the set of receivers (sinks), and R_t is the set of rates to the sinks. Considering the multicast connections in a lossy network using Random Linear Network Coding (RLNC) algorithm [8] that was established in literature to address such problem, then the following optimization problem for a lossy network is given as:

$$\min \xi(z)$$

subject to

$$z \in Z$$

$$\sum_{j\in K} x^t_{(iJj)} \le z_{iJK} b_{iJK}, \quad \forall (i,J) \in H,\ K \subset J, t \in T, x^t \in F^t \tag{2.1}$$

Also, considering similar multicast connections in a lossless network, then the optimization problem is given as:

$$\min \xi(z)$$

subject to

$$z \in Z$$

$$\sum_{j\in J} x^t_{(iJj)} \le z_{iJ}, \qquad \forall (i,J) \in H,\ t \in T, x^t \in F^t \tag{2.2}$$

where $x^t_{(iKk)}$ represents the average rate of packets that are injected on hyperarc *(i,K)* and received by exactly the set of nodes *K*, which occurs with average rate z_{iJK} and that allocated to a particular connection. Also $b_{iJK} = \frac{\sum_{\{N\subset K|N\cap L0\}} z_{iJN}}{z_{iK}}$ is the fraction of packets injected on hyperarc *(i,J)* received by a set of nodes that intersect K. Also, F^t is the bounded polyhedron of points x^t that satisfied the conservation of flow constraints [9].

In order to achieve the desired results, these problems were simplified further using various techniques and assumptions [10], [11]. For example, it is assumed that when nodes transmit in a lossless network, they reach all nodes in certain region, with cost increasing as the region expanded. This particular assumption is accepted because it is suitable for some applications such as minimising energy consumption problem which is being considered in this chapter. As a result, the problem was analysed and reduced to the case of linear separable cost and separable constraints. Then a fixed cost such as energy can be evaluated while the constraints set for Z are dropped. That is, suppose that $\xi(z) = \sum_{(i,K)\in H} a_{iK} z_{iK}$ where ξ_{iK} monotonically increasing while z_{iK} is varied, then, it is possible to achieve minimum energy multicast in a lossless wireless network without explicit regard for throughput or bandwidth. Therefore, a_{iK} is taken to represent the energy required to transmit a packet to nodes in K from node i. This process reduces the original problem into a linear optimisation problem with polynomial number of constraints that can be solved in polynomial time. However, as mentioned, solving the same problem using traditional or MIP method is NP-complete [12], [11].

2.2. Coded Packet Algorithm

Network coding is an alternative model for solving multicast problems. The approach is used to reduce multicast problem to a polynomial-time that can be solved by optimisation technique. An optimal subgraph in polynomial time could be found using a decentralised form of computation and based on this technique, a RLNC algorithm was derived [8][13]. The earlier algorithm using network coding approach is derived as Linear Network Coding (LNC) [9]. Although the LNC is sufficient for achieving the multicast capacity, however, in order to deploy network coding in a real time multicast network to achieve efficient results, RLNC algorithms are used [8]. The procedure for RLNC algorithm is summarised below.

- Initialisation of the source node that forms the message packets according to the same rules that the intermediate nodes are used to perform the operation.

- Operation at intermediate node is performed.
- If packet is received, Gaussian elimination is performed with the packets already in the buffer.
- For all outgoing edges, the intermediate node chooses all the packets that are in its buffer.
- Encoding operation is performed from the packet formed.
- Decoding operation at the sink nodes is performed from packet received.
- Gaussian elimination is performed with the packets already in the buffer.
- Inverse operation is performed and the sink node applies the inverse to the packets so as to obtain the message.

Interested readers are referred to [8] for detail about RLNC algorithm.

2.3. Performance Metric and Simulation Parameters

The performance metric considered for evaluation of minimum energy multicast using coded packet model is the energy-efficient, which is the function of multicast energy. In this work, multicast energy is considered as the cost of transmission of energy given a network sizes, the radius of connectivity, the dimension for the nodes, the source nodes and the receiving nodes using coded packet algorithm. In other words, a performance metric in terms of energy-efficient is investigated for coded packet network using RLNC algorithm. Multicast energy is considered as a cost in the multicast tree of different network sizes [14]. In order to evaluate the multicast energy performance, simulations are setup with the parameters configured for wireless networks. So the information about the source node, network size, dimension containing all nodes, radius of connectivity and the receiving nodes are specified as the input parameters. The energy associated with the multicast tree is computed using RLNC algorithm. Considering these settings, multicast energy of a particular wireless network can be computed. The average of the multicast energy is then evaluated.

In a broad review, the simulation is performed with minimum energy multicast framework in which communication nodes were placed randomly according to a uniform distribution over a (10×10)m and (50×50)m with a radius of connectivity of 3cm and 5cm to generate various network results. The average energy consumed by wireless multicast networks is evaluated.

The transmissions are subject to the distance of attenuation and zero interference is assumed. Therefore, when node i transmits, the signal-to-noise ratio (SNR) of the signal received at node J is $\mu d(i,J)^{-\alpha}$ where μ is an exponentially distributed random variable with unit mean, $d(i,J)$ represents the distance between node i and node J, and α represents an attenuation parameter that ranges between 2 and 4, and $\alpha = 2$ is assumed. Also, a threshold for SNR is denoted with β=0.25 such that $\mu d(i,j)^{-\alpha} \geq \beta$ implies a packet transmitted by node i is successfully received. In order to focus on the multicast energy, a stable condition in the transmission system is assumed.

Table 1.1. Mean of normalised multicast energy used to send multicast messages from a source node to receiver nodes {2, 3, 4, 5, 6, 7, 8, 9, 10} within randomly generated nodes {20, 30, 40} connected together with radius {3m, 5m} in {(10 × 10) m , (50 × 50) m} dimensions square

Average Multicast Energy						
Sink	***Radius = 3, Dimension = 10×10***			***Radius = 5, Dimension = 50×50***		
	20 nodes	***30 nodes***	***40 nodes***	***20 nodes***	***30 nodes***	***40 nodes***
2	4.50027	4.15490	3.14390	5.19479	3.60785	3.62417
3	5.46086	5.30356	4.60581	5.55607	5.1002	4.31278
4	6.22791	5.35979	4.75666	6.28641	5.56776	5.06807
5	6.81511	6.07549	4.75814	6.85942	5.87098	5.12135
6	7.32855	6.18796	5.56181	7.12087	6.09464	5.45237
7	7.23365	6.37327	5.58696	7.18488	6.76687	5.74148
8	8.10404	6.57230	6.25809	7.73925	6.62772	6.43736
9	8.81448	7.34824	6.29795	8.56634	7.14271	6.42996
10	8.45438	6.74705	6.30145	8.33395	7.12791	6.50145

2.4. Simulation Results

After all the parameters were set for the simulation, an output with name and path names is required. The output file contains information about the networks (the file that contains all the information about the nodes, how the nodes connect together and the link energy associate with each node). For example, the information in could read as start-node 0 is linked to an end-node 3000 with a link-cost or link energy of 7.999703767855737. This output file is then directed to the next procedure of the RLNC algorithm where the link-cost (energy) are extracted and the optimal value is obtained. The format to obtain the optimal solution is to specify the parameters for the computation as follows: total number of randomly generated nodes (--total), number of receiving nodes (--nodes), dimension occupied by the nodes (--dim), radius of connectivity (--rad) and the output filename (--file).

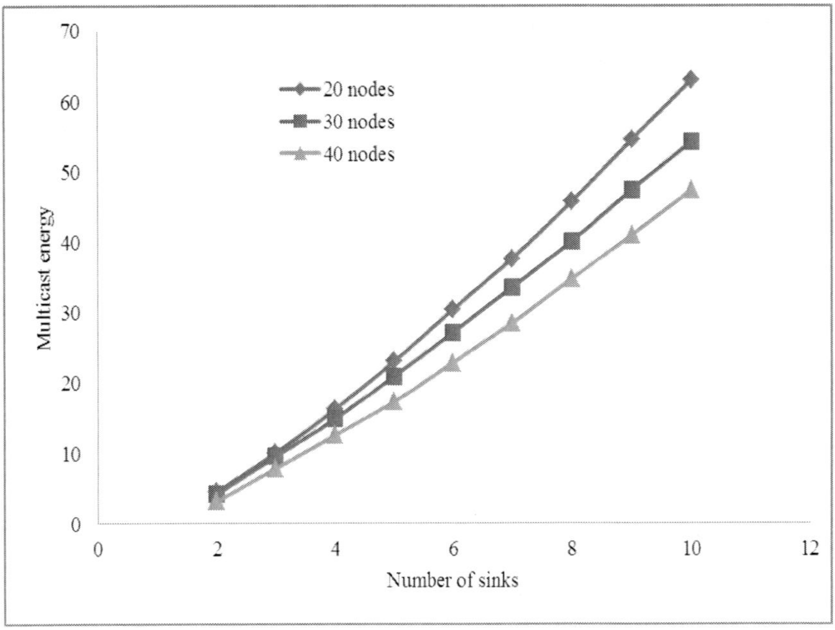

Figure 2. Cumulative of average multicast energy against the number of sinks for sending multicast message from a source node to receiver nodes 2,3,4,5,6,7,8,9 and 10 within randomly generated nodes 20,30 and 40 connected together with radius of 3m in 10×10m dimension square using RLNC algorithm for computation.

Next is to obtain results of the coded packet for minimum energy multicast computed by the RLNC algorithm. Table 1.1 presents the summarised results of the multicast energy computed by the RLNC algorithm. The Table shows the results of 20, 30 and 40 randomly generated nodes for 54 wireless networks with different parameters. That is, each entry represents results for a wireless network with varying network size and settings. The graphical interpretation of the cumulative results is presented in Figure 2.1 and Figure 2.3. Figure 2.1 represents the results with the following parameters: {Radius=3, Dimension=10×10m, Nodes=20,30,40, and Sinks=2,3,4,5,6,7,8,9,10}, while

Figure 2.2 represents the results with the following parameters: {Radius=5, Dimension=50×50m, Nodes=20,30,40, and Sinks=2,3,4,5,6,7,8,9,10}. The network size is defined as the number of nodes that are randomly generated, which are 20,30, and 40. Observe from the two figures that as the network size increases, the performance of RLNC algorithm in minimising energy is improved. A sample is taken from Figure 2.1 and the average multicast energy is evaluated for {Radius=3, Dimension=10, Nodes=20 and Sinks=2} as 4.50027. Also, the average multicast energy for {Radius=3, Dimension=10, Nodes=40 and Sinks=2} is 3.14390. That is, for the sampled 20 nodes and 40 nodes, the average multicast energy reduces from 4.50027 to 3.14390, with a difference of 1.35637.

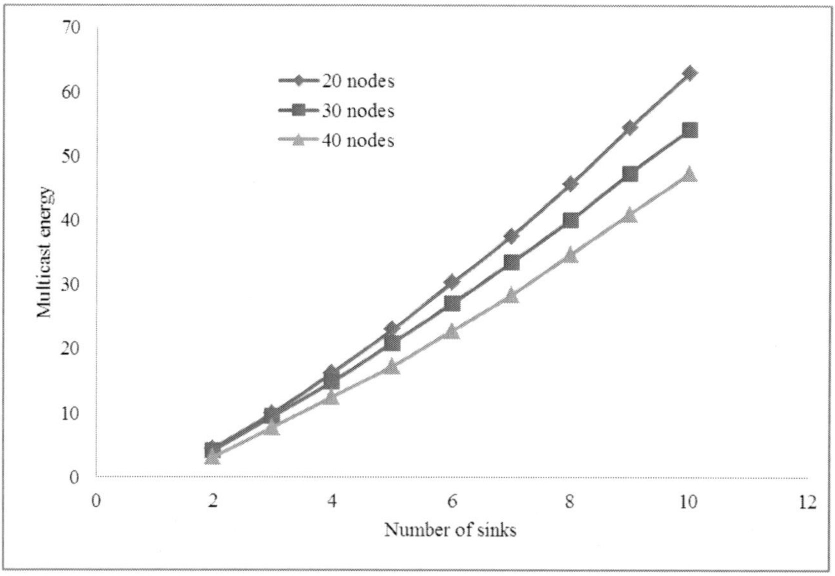

Figure 3. Cumulative of average multicast energy against the number of sinks for sending multicast message from a source node to receiver nodes 2,3,4,5,6,7,8,9 and 10 within randomly generated nodes 20,30 and 40 connected together with radius of 5m in 50×50m dimension square using RLNC algorithm for computation.

Observe from the result in Table 1.1, that the number of sinks have a serious impact in the network. For instance, the performance using RLNC algorithm reduces as the number of sinks increases. It means that the number of sinks is ultimately one of the factors that have to be taken seriously because it greatly affects the performance of the RLNC algorithm. Considering the sinks parameter, a sample from Table 1.1 is selected and the average multicast energy for {Radius=3, Dimension=10, Nodes=20 and Sinks=2} is calculated as 4.50027. Also, the average multicast energy for {Radius=3, Dimension=10, Nodes=20 and Sinks=4} is 6.22791. As for the sinks, the performance using RLNC algorithm degenerates as the number of sinks increases. The difference in average multicast energy for the sampled networks with 4 sinks is 1.72764.

3. The Empirical DEA Architecture and Models for Minimum Energy Multicast

Figure 3.1 summaries the proposed empirical DEA architecture for minimum energy multicast. The DEA model derived its dataset from the current coded packet model. As it could be observed from Figure3.1, the first part which is the coded packet model requires that the simulation is setup according to the minimum energy multicast framework using RLNC algorithm. The simulation is set with the algorithm requirements and the inputs parameters preconfigured. It should be noted that the results obtained from the simulation setup was presented in section 2.4. The second part of Figure 3.1 presents the empirical DEA models. The architecture consists of different components with the first component is about the multiple inputs and output data by the DMU transformation. Then the envelopment model is considered for the technical efficiency scores of DMUs. Subsequently, the slack model is considered for the identification of inefficient and weakly efficient networks. This component also suggests that the networks could be projected unto their efficient frontier or target. As a result, the target energy (minimum expected energy) of each network is evaluated and compared with the average energy computed by the RLNC algorithm. The differences in energy are computed by the energy gap component to find the energy saved.

In order to achieve this reduction in energy, the new DEA model is developed with assumption of input-orientation. In addition, this model was built upon CCR with the assumption of CRS. The model has envelopment and slack components and are summarized as follows:

(i) Envelopment Model – This model evaluate technical efficiency scores of each wireless network based on CCR/CRS assumptions
(ii) The Slack Model – This model project both inefficient and weak efficient wireless networks unto their efficient frontier based on CCR/CRS assumptions.

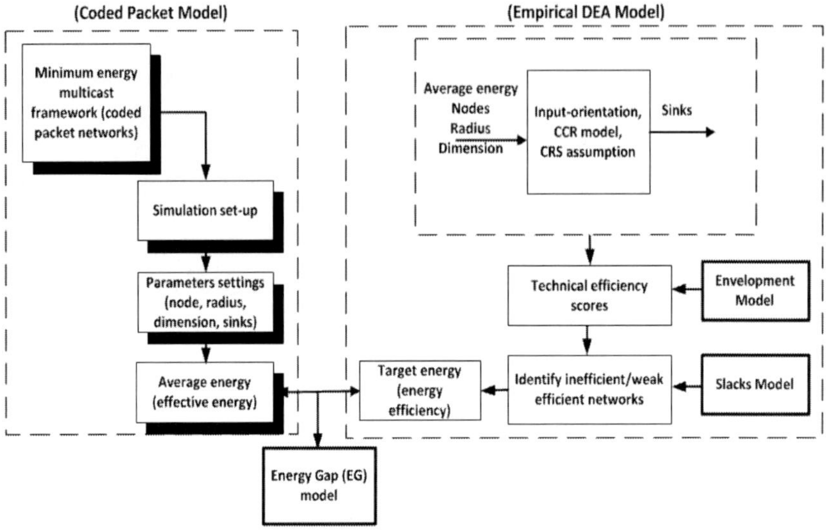

Figure 4. Architecture of the extended minimum energy multicast based on DEA models.

These models seek to evaluate TE, identify and project the inefficient and weak efficient unto their efficiency frontier. Eventually, the models minimize multicast energy through linear programming techniques obtained from *ratio problem*. Note that the minimum energy achieved does not affect the output results. In other words, these models keep the current empirical level of outputs constant and minimizes the inputs (energy).

3.1. Ratio Problems

This section explores the technical efficiency evaluation through Mathematical approach. Since technical efficiency evaluation is classified as ratio problem then, there is a need to express the variables in this form. This approach to ratio problems optimisation is known as efficiency ratio from where envelopment and slack models are derived [15], [16]. This work considered five indexes with four inputs and one output, and applied efficiency ratio approach to these indexes, then the inputs and outputs in terms of ratio problem is defined. Thus the weights required for model development is constructed through the following expression:

$$\frac{u(g)}{v_1(e)+v_2(d)+v_3(r)+v_4(z)},$$

where u denotes the weight for the output, and v_1, v_2, v_3 and v_4 are weight for the inputs. Also, the sinks are denoted with letter *g*, the multicast energy with letter *e*, the dimension with letter *d*, and radius with letter *r* while *z* represents the number of nodes in the network. This ratio is evaluated for each of the wireless network, which is denoted with notation DMU. The ratio problem technique performs optimisation by finding the maximum efficiency that a wireless network achieved under a set of weights. These set of weights then provide optimal value that efficiency ratio achieved from *n* observations. In this case, 54 wireless networks are considered. The expectation is to determine the efficient frontier or best practice frontier for these 54 wireless networks. It is assumed that the input and the output are all non-negative data. The wireless networks that are able to reduce their average energy to the expected minimum are said to attain efficiency frontier or operating based on best practice.

In order to develop appropriate model for all the 54 networks, the efficiency ratio is established considering a set of n observations for the DMUs where each observation, $DMU_j \{j=1,2,\ldots,n\}$ uses n multiple inputs x_{ij} $(i=1,2,\ldots,m)$ to produces multiple outputs y_{rj} $(r=1,2,\ldots,s)$. The variable x_{ij} represents the vector of inputs into DMU_{ij} and y_{rj} represents the corresponding vector of outputs. Then, the efficiency ratio for DMU_j can be expressed as:

$$\frac{\sum_{r=1}^{s} u_r y_{rj}}{\sum_{i=1}^{m} v_i x_{ij}} = \frac{u_1 y_{1j} + u_2 y_{2j} + \ldots + u_s y_{sj}}{v_1 x_{1j} + v_2 x_{2j} + \ldots + v_m x_{mj}} \tag{3.1}$$

where $u_r\,(r=1,2,\ldots,s)\,and\ v_i\,(i=1,2,\ldots,m)$ are unknown weights. This ratio accounts for all outputs and inputs. The weights assigned to each input and each output is used as variables in the optimisation process. Furthermore, considering maximising a particular wireless network (DMU_0), then the maximised efficiency:

$$max\frac{\sum_{r=1}^{s}u_r y_{r0}}{\sum_{i=1}^{m}v_i x_{io}}=\frac{u_1 y_{1o}+u_2 y_{2o}+\ldots+u_s y_{so}}{v_1 x_{1o}+v_2 x_{2o}+\ldots+v_m x_{mo}} \quad (3.2)$$

could be achieved, but the maximisation problem(3.2) is unbounded and therefore required additional constraints. One of the constraints is to assume a set of normalisation, one for each DMU. Another condition is that the virtual output to virtual input ratio of every DMU must be less than or equal to unity.

3.2. The Envelopment Model

3.2.1. Model Development

In dealing with ratio problem, an effective technique to consider in solving such optimisation is the Linear Programming (LP), a framework that is paramount to optimisation problems. The goal here is to develop models that are appropriate for minimisation of energy problem using LP framework [16]. This process will explore the DEA methodology based on efficiency ratio approach to determine a set of weights that yields the maximum efficiency ratio. Thus the following optimisation problems are considered:

$$maximise\frac{\sum_{r=1}^{s}u_r y_{r0}}{\sum_{i=1}^{m}v_i x_{i0}}$$

Subject to:

$$\frac{\sum_{r=1}^{s}u_r y_{rj}}{\sum_{i=1}^{m}v_i x_{ij}}\leq 1, j=1,2,\ldots,n$$

$$u_r, v_i \geq 0 \; (r=1,2,\ldots,s) \text{ and } v_i \, (i=1,2,\ldots,m) \quad (3.3)$$

The DMU_o is then maximised using efficiency ratio model (3.3), and can be generalised for all the DMU_s. In other words, the above model (3.3) can be used to calculate the efficiency of a specific member of a given set of n

DMU_s subject to a condition that the efficiency ratings or scores of each DMU should not exceed 1. However, model (3.3) is in fractional form that is a non-linear programming model. Consequently, model (3.3) in its present form is difficult to solve. Hence, a transformation is required. The approach to convert model (3.3) into an equivalent linear problem form was established and presented in [17]. Considering this transformation technique, model (3.3) is rewritten as:

$$Max\, z = \sum_{r=1}^{s} \mu_r y_{r0}$$

Subject to

$$\sum_{r=1}^{s} \mu_r y_{rj} - \sum_{i=1}^{m} v_i x_{ij} \leq 0, \quad j = 1, 2, \ldots, n$$

$$\sum_{i=1}^{m} v_i x_{i0} = 1$$

$$\mu_r, v_i \geq 0 \tag{3.4}$$

where μ_r *and* v_i are decision variables and denoted output and input multipliers respectively. This type of formation represented by model (3.4) is a multiplier, which its objective function is the weighted sum of outputs for DMU_o under evaluation. Again, the first set of n constraints specifies that each efficiency rating cannot be greater than 1. The constraint $\sum_{i=1}^{m} v_i x_{i0} = 1$ is a normalization condition.

3.2.2. Input-oriented CCR/CRS Model

Model (3.4) appears computational intensive and for this reason it could be solved in its dual form. In addition, consider the type of orientation suitable for the optimisation problem and carefully formulate appropriate model toward that assumption. That is, the goal of this work is to minimise the inputs while the outputs are kept at their current levels. A suitable approach for such scenario is the input-orientation. With this approach, inputs variables are controlled. In order to achieve input minimisation (e.g., energy), the dual of model (3.4) is modified and the derivation is given below.

$$\theta^* = min\ \theta$$

Subject to

$$\sum_{j=1}^{n} \lambda_j x_{ij} \leq \theta x_{i0}, \qquad i = 1,2,\ldots,m;$$

$$\sum_{j=1}^{n} \lambda_j y_{rj} \geq y_{r0}, \qquad r = 1,2,\ldots,s;$$

$$\lambda_j \geq 0, \qquad j = 1,2,\ldots,n, \qquad (3.5)$$

where λ_j are unknown weights with $j = 1,2,\ldots,n$ and they correspond to the DMU numbers. DMU_0 is one of the n DMU under evaluation, and θx_{i0} and y_{r0} are the ith input and r^{th} output for DMU_0 respectively. Model (3.5) is the expected input-oriented CCR with constant returns to scale (CRS) envelopment model.

3.2.3. Conditions for Efficiency Ratings

The following definitions or conditions are responsible for efficiency ratings or scores classification of DMUs:

If $\theta^* = 1$, *then the DMU under evaluation is a frontier point (efficient), that is, no other* DMU_s *operates more efficiently than this DMU. Otherwise if* $\theta^* < 1$, *then the DMU under evaluation is inefficient, that is, this DMU can either increase its output levels or decrease its input levels to achieve efficiency* [18]. The θ^* represents the efficiency score of DMU_o based on input-orientation meaning the model assumes that DMU_s are able to linearly scale the inputs without affecting the performance. In other words, the input values (e.g., energy) are minimised while maintaining the current output levels. Application of this to the network assume that wireless network can maintain its number of multicast messages to selected number of sinks (output) while decreasing its input resources (e.g., energy) so as to become one of the best networks.

3.3. The Slack Models

3.3.1. Slack for the Input-oriented CCR/CRS Model

In additional to model (3.5), the slacks model is needed to push the inefficient DMUs to their real optimal efficiency so that expected minimum energy could be achieved. This is necessary provided that a DMU cannot reach its efficiency frontier that is optimal point after proportional reductions in inputs using model (3.5). In order to obtain the slacks in DEA methodology, a second stage linear programming model is required to be solved after the dual linear programming model (3.5). This second stage linear programming model formulated for slack values is as follows:

$$max \sum_{i=1}^{m} s_j^- + \sum_{r=1}^{s} s_r^+$$

Subject to

$$\sum_{j=1}^{n} \lambda_j x_{ij} + s_j^- = \theta^* x_{io}, \qquad i = 1,2,\ldots,\text{m};$$

$$\sum_{j=1}^{n} \lambda_j y_{rj} - s_r^+ = y_{r0}, \qquad r = 1,2,\ldots,\text{s};$$

$$j \geq 0 \qquad j = 1,2,\ldots,n \qquad (3.6)$$

where s_j^- *and* s_r^+ represent input and output slacks respectively. The superscripts (-) and (+) represent input reduction and output augmentation respectively. Here, θ^* is the efficiency score resulted from the initial run of model (3.5).

3.3.2. Slack Conditions and the Gap

It is possible that the solution obtained from model (3.5) and (3.6) contains weak efficient DMUs that give rise to multiple optimal solutions. This also affects the performance of DMUs. Therefore, the following conditions help to identify full and weak efficiency status of DMUs [19], [20]:

Condition for Fully Efficient DMUs: DMU_0 is fully (100%) efficient if and only if both (i) $\theta^* = 1$ and (ii) all slacks $s_i^{(-*)} = s_r^{(+*)} = 0$. In other words, full (100%) efficiency is attained by any DMU if and only if none of its inputs or outputs can be improved without worsening some of its other inputs or outputs.

Condition for Weakly Efficient DMUs: DMU_0 is weakly efficient if and only if both (i) $\theta^* = 1$ and (ii) $s_i^{-*} \neq 0$ and/or $s_r^{+*} \neq 0$ for some *I* and r in some alternate optima.

The presence of inefficient DMUs as well as weak efficient DMUs leads to another Mathematical expression to calculate the set of input and output targets that would make an inefficient or weak efficient DMUs to become fully efficient. The level of efficient target for inputs and outputs can be calculated using the following relations:

$$\begin{cases} X^*_{i0} = \theta^* x_{io} - S_i^{-*}, & i=1,2,\ldots,m \\ Y^*_{r0} = y_{ro} + S_r^{+*}, & r=1,2,\ldots,s \end{cases} \tag{3.7}$$

Efficient target can be calculated taking for instance the target for the input values, then the input values (e.g., average multicast energy) are multiplied with an optimal efficiency score (θ^*), and slack amounts are subtracted. The gap is evaluated by subtracting the target results from the input values (e.g., average multicast energy).

4. Empirical DEA Results

4.1. DEA Tools

The Technical Efficiency (TE) is evaluated using DEA software, which is the tool that was specially packaged to solve the envelopment model and other types of DEA models. The DEA library includes the DEA-Solver and LP solver (linear programming solver) to perform optimisations. Examples of the DEA tool are packages like DEAP (DEA program), Warwick DEA, ON-Front and DEAOS (Data Envelopment Analysis Online Software). In addition, DEA tool is available as open source software online. However, this work makes use of DEAOS for the implementation of the models. Furthermore, the DEAOS is available as online software [21]. The readers are referred to [21] for details about the DEAOS package and user's documentation. The DEA implementation procedures are as follows: formulating the DEA Problem, setting the variables, configuring the DEA forms, solving the DEA problem, exporting and extracting the solutions from the excel files. The analysis of results is presented in the next section.

4.2. Analysis of Results

4.2.1. TE Scores for Input-oriented CCR/CRS Envelopment Model

In this section, model (3.5) is solved using the DEAOS then the Technical Efficiency (TE) scores are extracted from the "Efficiency" sheet of the DEA solver. As noted in section 3.2, the function of envelopment model is to evaluate the efficiency of each of the wireless network called DMU and compare with all other wireless network (DMUs).

It identifies those DMUs that are operating inefficiently as compared with other DMUs' actual operating results. It accomplishes this by locating the best practice DMUs and then evaluates the magnitude of inefficiency of the inefficient DMUs compared to the best practice DMUs. The best practice DMUs are relatively efficient and are identified by a DEA efficiency rating of $\theta = 1$. The inefficient DMUs are identified by an efficiency rating of less than 1 ($\theta < 1$). Table 4.1 provides the extraction of the efficiency of all the DMU from the "Efficiency" sheet computed by the DEA solver. Column two of Table 4.1 presents the results of DEA TE scores of all the 54 wireless networks (DMUs). Column three of Table 4.1 also presents the TE scores in their percentages.

Table 4.1. Efficiency scores and slacks reports for input-oriented CCR/CRS DEA model

	Measurements			Input Slacks			
DMU	Efficiency Scores	TE(%)	TIE(%)	Ave. energy	Dimension	Radius	Nodes
DMU_1	0.2999126	30.0	70.0	0	0.9921306	0.2993879	0
DMU_2	0.4008414	40.1	59.9	0	0	0	0
DMU_3	0.4920725	49.2	50.8	0	0	0	0
DMU_4	0.5798874	58.0	42.0	0	0	0	0
DMU_5	0.6627010	66.3	33.7	0	0	0	0
DMU_6	0.7800223	78.0	22.0	0	0	0	0
DMU_7	0.8242685	82.4	17.6	0	0	0	0
DMU_8	0.900000	90.0	10.0	0.32409	0	0	0
DMU_9	1	100.0	0.0	0	0	0	0
DMU_{10}	0.2750224	27.5	72.5	0	9.7529166	0	0
DMU_{11}	0.3954612	39.5	60.5	0	12.409958	0	0
DMU_{12}	0.4865748	48.7	51.3	0	11.254727	0	0
DMU_{13}	0.5734824	57.3	42.7	0	9.5527109	0	0
DMU_{14}	0.6707014	67.1	32.9	0	9.1911873	0	0
DMU_{15}	0.7776498	77.8	22.2	0	10.094469	0	0
DMU_{16}	0.8435955	84.4	15.6	0	5.6674165	0	0
DMU_{17}	0.9000000	90.0	10.0	0.209151	0	0	0
DMU_{18}	1	100.0	0.0	0	0	0	0
DMU_{19}	0.3033262	30.3	69.7	0	0	0.3099786	0

Measurements				Input Slacks			
DMU	Efficiency Scores	TE (%)	TIE (%)	Ave. energy	Dimension	Radius	Nodes
DMU_{20}	0.3652144	36.5	63.5	0	0	0.1956432	0
DMU_{21}	0.4828637	48.3	51.7	0	0	0.2485910	0
DMU_{22}	0.5453004	54.5	45.5	0	0	0.1359013	0
DMU_{23}	0.6445800	64.5	35.5	0	0	0.1337401	0
DMU_{24}	0.7339356	73.4	26.6	0	0	0	0
DMU_{25}	0.8176758	81.8	18.2	0	0	0	0
DMU_{26}	0.9000000	90.0	10.0	0.541071	0	0	0
DMU_{27}	1	100.0	0.0	0	0	0	0
DMU_{28}	0.3493188	34.9	65.1	0	15.465942	0	2.4795654
DMU_{29}	0.3767524	37.7	62.3	0	0	0	0
DMU_{30}	0.4683195	46.8	53.2	0	19.415974	0	0
DMU_{31}	0.5607725	56.1	43.9	0	0	0	0
DMU_{32}	0.6526743	65.3	34.7	0	26.633716	0	0
DMU_{33}	0.6987965	69.9	30.1	0	27.795397	0	0
DMU_{34}	0.8119862	81.2	18.8	0	32.599308	0	0
DMU_{35}	0.8700847	87.0	13.0	0	30.914400	0	0
DMU_{36}	0.9679643	96.8	3.2	0	34.553930	0	0
DMU_{37}	0.4008683	40.1	59.9	0	0	0.6026050	8.0347339
DMU_{38}	0.4104457	41.0	59.0	0	0	0.3313372	4.4178288

Table 4.1. Continued

Measurements				Input Slacks			
DMU	Efficiency Scores	TE (%)	TIE (%)	Ave. energy	Dimension	Radius	Nodes
DMU_{39}	0.5299054	53.0	47.0	0	0	0.3897163	5.1962175
DMU_{40}	0.6621758	66.2	33.8	0	0	0.4865273	6.4870306
DMU_{41}	0.6797913	68.0	32.0	0	0	0.2393739	3.1916516
DMU_{42}	0.7895197	79.0	21.0	0	0	0.2685591	3.5807881
DMU_{43}	0.8055429	80.6	19.4	0	0	0.0166287	0.2217162
DMU_{44}	0.9005002	90.1	9.9	0	0	0.0015005	0.0200065
DMU_{45}	1	100.0	0.0	0	0	0	0
DMU_{46}	0.3477458	34.8	65.2	0	15.387291	0	5.9098331
DMU_{47}	0.4383333	43.8	56.2	0	0	0	5.5333312
DMU_{48}	0.4973451	49.7	50.3	0	20.867257	0	3.8938057
DMU_{49}	0.6152138	61.5	38.5	0	25.760688	0	4.6085505
DMU_{50}	0.6934361	69.3	30.7	0	28.671803	0	3.7374426
DMU_{51}	0.7682714	76.8	23.2	0	31.413571	0	2.7308569
DMU_{52}	0.7867724	78.7	21.3	0	31.338618	0	0
DMU_{53}	0.8859165	88.6	11.4	0	35.295824	0	0
DMU_{54}	0.9758566	97.6	2.4	0	0	0	0

Observe from Table 4.1 that only DMU_9, DMU_{18}, DMU_{27} and DMU_{45} have efficiency scores of $\theta = 1$ (i.e., 100%) and thus they are identified as efficient. Other DMUs have efficiency scores of less than 1 ($\theta < 1$) but greater than 0, and thus they are identified as inefficient. In order to visually understand how the efficiency scores are distributed, Figure 4.1 presents the efficiency scores against each of the DMUs. Note that the inefficient DMUs can improve their TE scores. For example, DMU_1 can improve its TE score by reducing certain inputs up to 70% (100 - 30). Similarly, DMU_2 can do so with approximately 59.9% input reduction. However, DMU_{36} is closer to an efficiency frontier, and needs only a 3.2% reduction of its input resources. This analysis is the technical inefficiency of the DMUs and the results is presented as a percentage in column four of Table 4.1.

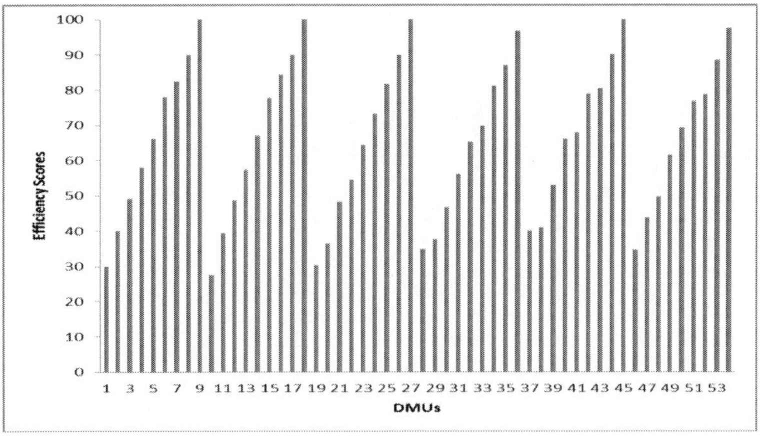

Figure 4.1. Distribution of technical efficiency scores of 54 wireless networks computed by envelopment for musing the input-oriented CCR/CRS model.

4.2.2. Slack Results for Input-oriented CCR/CRS Model

Model (3.6) represented the Mathematical derivation of slacks with CRS assumption. In this section, the results of the model are analysed and evaluated for projection/target in wireless networks. The function of the model is to use the slack values as a function to determine those wireless networks that will be projected unto efficient frontier and compared the values with the coded packet model. The slacks computed by the DEA solver and which is extracted from the "Slack" sheet of the DEA solver are reported in columns five, six, seven and eight of Table 4.1. Important properties needed for the evaluation of slacks is presented in section 3.3.2. Using these conditions, it is observed that none of the efficient DMUs have a slack, meaning that slacks exist only for those DMUs identified as inefficient.

Table 4.2. Results of the average multicast energy computed by coded packet (RLNC) model, the projected multicast energy computed by the proposed input-oriented CCR/CRS model and energy saved

DMU	Average energy (Coded packet Model)	Projected energy (CCR/CRS DEA Model)	EG Model (Energy saved)
DMU_1	4.50027	1.349687509	3.1505825
DMU_2	5.46086	2.188938801	3.2719212
DMU_3	6.22791	3.064583502	3.1633265
DMU_4	6.81511	3.951996460	2.8631135
DMU_5	7.32855	4.856637563	2.4719124
DMU_6	7.23365	5.642407952	1.5912420
DMU_7	8.10404	6.679904730	1.4241353
DMU_8	8.81448	7.608942000	1.205538
DMU_9	8.45438	8.454380000	0
DMU_{10}	5.19479	1.428683796	3.7661062
DMU_{11}	5.55607	2.197210195	3.3588598
DMU_{12}	6.28641	3.058808829	3.2276012
DMU_{13}	6.85942	3.933756586	2.9256634
DMU_{14}	7.12087	4.775977768	2.3448922
DMU_{15}	7.18488	5.587320197	1.5975598
DMU_{16}	7.73925	6.528796565	1.2104534
DMU_{17}	8.56634	7.500555000	1.0657850
DMU_{18}	8.33395	8.333950000	0
DMU_{19}	4.1549	1.260290000	2.8946100
DMU_{20}	5.30356	1.936936409	3.3666236
DMU_{21}	5.35979	2.588047851	2.7717421
DMU_{22}	6.07549	3.312967372	2.7625226
DMU_{23}	6.18796	3.988635421	2.1993246
DMU_{24}	6.37327	4.677569864	1.6957001
DMU_{25}	6.57230	5.374010935	1.1982891
DMU_{26}	7.34824	6.072345000	1.2758950
DMU_{27}	6.74705	6.747050000	0

DMU	Average energy (Coded packet Model)	Projected energy (CCR/CRS DEA Model)	EG Model (Energy saved)
DMU_{28}	3.60785	1.260290000	2.3475600
DMU_{29}	5.1002	1.921512433	3.1786876
DMU_{30}	5.56776	2.607490509	2.9602695
DMU_{31}	5.87098	3.292284287	2.5786957
DMU_{32}	6.09464	3.977814978	2.1168250
DMU_{33}	6.76687	4.728664738	2.0382053
DMU_{34}	6.62772	5.381616903	1.2461031
DMU_{35}	7.14271	6.214762736	0.9279473
DMU_{36}	7.12791	6.899562380	0.2283476
DMU_{37}	3.14390	1.260290000	1.8836100
DMU_{38}	4.60581	1.890435000	2.7153750
DMU_{39}	4.75666	2.520580000	2.2360800
DMU_{40}	4.75814	3.150725000	1.6074150
DMU_{41}	5.56181	3.780870000	1.7809400
DMU_{42}	5.58696	4.411015000	1.1759450
DMU_{43}	6.25809	5.041160000	1.2169300
DMU_{44}	6.29795	5.671305000	0.6266450
DMU_{45}	6.30145	6.301450000	0
DMU_{46}	3.62417	1.260290000	2.3638800
DMU_{47}	4.31278	1.890435000	2.4223450
DMU_{48}	5.06807	2.520580000	2.5474900
DMU_{49}	5.12135	3.150725000	1.9706250
DMU_{50}	5.45237	3.780870000	1.6715000
DMU_{51}	5.74148	4.411015000	1.3304650
DMU_{52}	6.43736	5.064736940	1.3726231
DMU_{53}	6.42996	5.696407480	0.7335525
DMU_{54}	6.50145	6.344483131	0.1569669

The slack model is used to complement the envelopment model. Thus, slacks are obtained after proportional reductions of inputs i.e., after the envelopment model was executed. Slack computation is necessary especially when a DMU cannot reach its efficiency frontier (target). Slacks are needed to project such inefficient and weakly efficient DMUs, for instance, DMU8 is required to reduce its average energy consumption using slack value of approximately 0.32409. Similarly, DMU_{17} and DMU_{26} required reducing its average energy consumption using slack value of 0.209151 and 0.541071 respectively. However, DMU_1 requires two input reduction with the following slack values: the dimension (0.9921306), and radius (0.2993879) to become efficient.

The target analysis is carried out for each DMU where target input levels are prescribed. These targets are the function of respective slack values that are added to inputs. The target calculation is computed by model (3.7). The model calculates the targets values by multiplied the input value (average multicast energy) with the optimal efficiency score, and then slack are subtracted from this amount. Results of the projected (targeted) energy together with the results obtained from simulated coded packet model are presented in Table 4.2. As shown in the Table, the projected energy represented the expected optimal energy if all the DMUs operated efficiently. In order to evaluate the target energy, weak efficient and inefficient wireless networks (DMUs) are identified together with their efficiency scores and slacks.

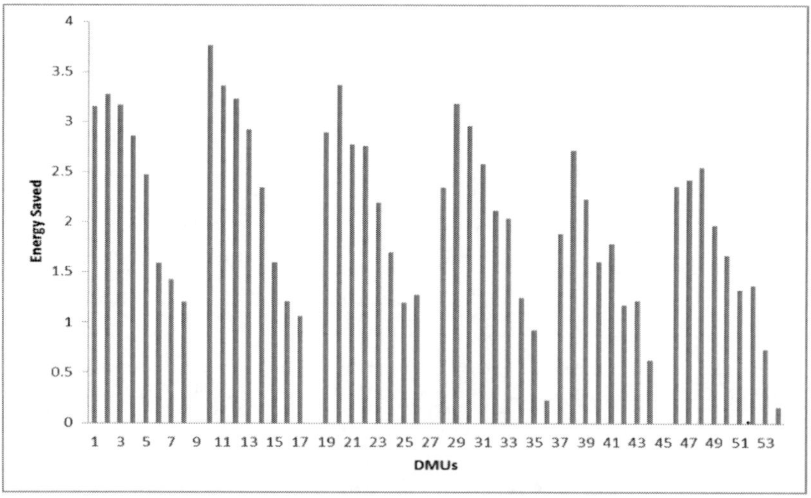

Figure 4.2. Energy saved by individual wireless networks using input-oriented CCR/CRS DEA model.

4.2.3. Energy Gap for Input-oriented CCR/CRS

As mentioned earlier, the empirical DEA architecture also incorporates the energy gap (EG) component. The EG consider the result obtained from the coded packet and DEA models, and then finds the difference between the two models. Column four of Table 4.2 presents the EG results for the input-oriented CCR/CRS model. Observe from the table that the EG computes the difference between the average multicast energy of the coded packet model and the proposed empirical DEA model. This difference is the amount of the energy saved if the wireless networks operate efficiently. For example, as could be observed from Table 4.2, the energy saved if DMU_1 operates efficiently is 3.1505825 and the energy saved if DMU_2 operates efficiently is 3.2719212. Figure 4.2 presents the graphical view of the energy saved by individual wireless network. As it is shown, DMU_{10} has the highest energy saved which is 3.7661062 followed by DMU_{20} with the value equal 3.3666236. The DMUs that satisfy slack conditions presented in section 3.3.2 are not needed to save energy because they have already fully operated efficiently. These DMUs are DMU_9, DMU_{18}, DMU_{27} and DMU_{45}.

5. Energy Saved

This section discusses the results of two techniques by which multicast energy is minimised in wireless networks if they operate efficiently. The two models demonstrated the ability to further save multicast energy in wireless networks. Remember that performances of these models are based on different methodology and assumptions. In this section, the performance of input-oriented CCR/CRS model in terms of energy saved is compared with the coded packet model. The amount of energy saved by the input-oriented CCR/CRS model is evaluated. This is obtained by finding the difference between the total average multicast energy and the total projected energy. As could be evaluated from Table 4.2, the total energy saved is the total average multicast energy (329.77019) minus total projected multicast energy (227.5317618). The difference is equal to 102.23843, the total energy saved. Figure 5.1 represents the total energy saved, the total target energy and the total average energy. This reduction in energy as demonstrated by the CCR/CRS DEA model is huge compare to the coded packet model approach. Observe from Figure 5.1 that the difference between the coded packet model and the empirical DEA model is the energy gap. This gap between the two models represents the amount of energy saved if the wireless networks function efficiently.

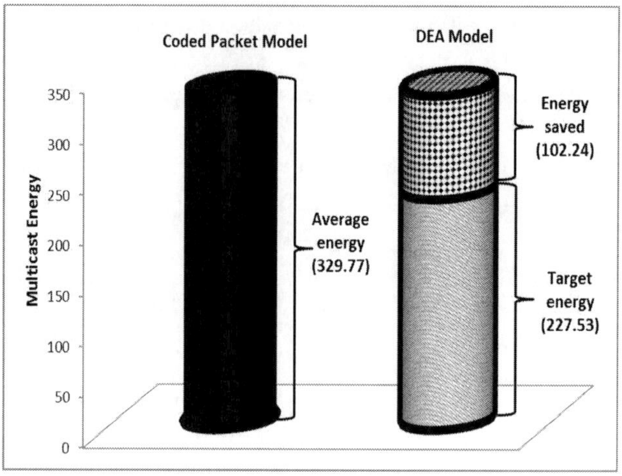

Figure 5.1. Total target energy and the total energy saved using input-oriented CCR/CRS DEA model based on frontier production function.

Conclusion

This chapter studied the current minimum energy multicast framework and investigated the performance of the coded packet technique for minimum energy multicast. Simulation results have shown that coded packet method is sub-optimal and the mode of evaluation adopted was based on effective performance. While effective performance is a good evaluation tool, it is not enough to measure the efficiency of networks appropriately. In order to adequately evaluate the network efficiency a multi-criteria decision with multiple inputs and multiple outputs using DEA technique was considered. With this approach, the expected minimum (optimal) energy multicast in wireless networks was achieved.

The main objective of this work was to design an empirical DEA architecture for minimum energy multicast to evaluate the energy efficiency of wireless multicast networks. The aim of the design is to minimise the amount of energy consumed by the networks nodes without affecting their performance. As a result, DEA methodology was explored. Specifically, three models were formulated for minimum energy in wireless multicast networks. These include envelopment model for the evaluation of technical efficiency, the slack model for projection of weak efficient or inefficient networks unto the efficient frontier, and energy gap (EG) model for evaluation of energy saved. The envelopment model was formulated as the input-oriented CCR assuming constant returns to scale. This was extended to accommodate the slack variables. The energy gap model is a simple Mathematical expression that finds the different between the value of the coded packet model and the DEA model after projection. It was discovered that DEA model outperformed the coded packet model. Thus the DEA model was able to save substantial amount of energy if the wireless networks operate efficiently.

References

[1] Blume, O; Zeller, D; Barth, U. "Approaches to energy efficient wireless access networks," in *4th international symposium on communications, control, and signal processing*, 2010.

[2] Ho, T; Lun, DS. *Network Coding: An Introduction.* Cambridge University Press, 2008.

[3] Uddin, M; Talha, M; Azizah, S. Abdul Rahman Asadullah, and J. Memon, Jameel Ahmed Khader, "Green Information Technology (IT) framework for energy efficient data centers using virtualization," *Int. J. Phys. Sci;* vol. 7, no. 13, 2052 – 2065, 2012.

[4] Mueen U; Azizah, AR. "Virtualization Implementation Model for Cost Effective and Efficient Data Centers," *Int. J. Adv. Comput. Sci. Appl*, vol. 2, no. 1, 59–68, 2011.

[5] Reviriego, P; Christensen, K; Rabanillo, J; Maestro, J. "Performance evaluation of energy efficient ethernet," *IEEE Commun. Lett*, vol. 13, no. 9, 1–3, 2009.

[6] Ajibesin, AA; Ventura, N; Murgu, A; Chan, H. "Data envelopment analysis: Efficient technique for measuring performance of wireless network coding protocols," in *15th International Conference on Advanced Communication Technology*, 2013, 1122–1127.

[7] Fragouli, C. Soljanin, E. "Network Coding Applications, Foundation and Trends in Networking," vol. 2, no. 2, 135–269, 2007.

[8] Ho, T; Medard, M; Koetter, R; Karger, DR; Effros, M; Shi, J; Leong, B. "A Random Linear Network Coding Approach to Multicast," *IEEE Trans. Inf. Theory*, vol. 52, no. 10, 4413–4430, Oct. 2006.

[9] Li, S.-YR; Yeung, RW; Cai, N. "Linear network coding," *IEEE Trans. Inform. Theory*, vol. 49, no. 2, 371–381, 2003.

[10] Lun, DS; Ratnakar, N; Medard, M; Koetter, R; Karger, DR; Ho, T; Ahmed, E. "Minimum-cost multicast over coded packet networks," *IEEE Trans. Inf. Theory*, vol. 52, no. 6, 2608–2623, Jun. 2006.

[11] Lun, D; Médard, M; Ho, T; Koetter, R. "Network coding with a cost criterion," *Proceeding Int. Symp. Inf. Theory its Appl*, 2004.

[12] Wieselthier, EJ; Nguyen, GD; Anthony, E. "Algorithms for energy-efficient multicasting in static ad hoc wireless networks," *Mob. Networks Appl*, vol. 6, no. 3, 251–263, 2001.

[13] Li, Z; and Li, B. "Network Coding in Undirected Networks," *Computer (Long. Beach. Calif)*, 1–6, 2004.

[14] Ajibesin, AA; Ventura, N; Murgu, A; Chan, HA. "Cost-efficient multicast over coded packet wireless networks using data envelopment analysis," in *2013 IEEE 10th Consumer Communications and Networking Conference (CCNC)*, 2013, 546–551.

[15] Emrouznejad, A; Cabanda, E. "An aggregate measure of financial ratios using a multiplicative DEA model. International," *J. Financ. Serv. Manag*, vol. 4, no. 2, 114–126, 2010.

[16] Cullinane, K; Song, D-W; Wang, T. "The Application of Mathematical Programming Approaches to Estimating Container Port Production Efficiency," *J. Product. Anal*, vol. 24, no. 1, 73–92, Sep. 2005.

[17] Banker, WW; Charnes, R.D; Cooper, A; "Some models for the estimation of technical and scale inefficiencies in Data Envelopment Analysis," *Manage. Sci*, vol. 30, no. 9, 1078–1092, 1984.

[18] Cooper, WW; Lawrence, MS; Joe, Z. *Handbook on data envelopment analysis*, 2nd edn. Springer Science+ Business Media, 2011.

[19] Cooper, WW; Lawrence, MS; Kaoru, T. *Data envelopment analysis: a comprehensive text with models, applications, references and DEA-solver software*. Springer, 2007.

[20] Tone, K. "A slacks-based measure of efficiency in data envelopment analysis," *Eur. J. Oper. Res*, vol. 130, no. 3, 498–509, 2001.

[21] "Data Envelopment Analysis," 2015. [Online]. Available: http://www.deaos.com/. [Accessed: 25-March 2015].

In: Network Coding and Data Compression
Editor: MaryAnn Simmons
ISBN: 978-1-63483-185-7
© 2015 Nova Science Publishers, Inc.

Chapter 5

MODELING OF PHYSICAL LAWS BY COMPRESSED EXPERIMENTAL DATA

Igor Grabec[*]
Amanova Ltd, Ljubljana, Slovenia

Abstract

A physical law can be most generally experimentally modeled by the probability distribution of measured variables. For this purpose the kernel estimator determined by experimental samples of variables is applicable. When experimental samples are overwhelming it is reasonable to use less numerous prototype samples. In this case a prototype represents experimental samples taking place in its surrounding. In our treatment the interval of the surrounding is described by the standard deviation of instrument output scattering at calibration. An algorithm is then proposed for creation of prototypes and their adaptation to experimental samples that yields a proper model. This process is quantitatively characterized by changes of the cost function that is expressed by the information entropy. The number of created prototypes is generally much smaller than the number of experimental samples although the information provided by experimental data is well preserved. The compression procedure is demonstrated on analytically determined chaotic data and measured samples of traffic flow. Its performance is characterized by various information statistics.

[*] E-mail address: igor.grabec@fs.uni-lj.si

1. Introduction

Monitoring and characterization of very complex phenomena having stochastic character is usually performed by electronic data acquisition systems. As a characteristic example we mention here a traffic flow on roads of various countries, whose properties are specified by measurements performed by networks of counters (Treiber et al., 2013). Due to complexity of traffic the measured data are overwhelming and there generally appears a question how to store and present them efficiently. Merely by intuition, one could suggest to use for this purpose a set of prototype data that properly represent the properties of experimental samples. However, the problem is to specify prototypes so that they could be estimated automatically in an information processing system. We expect that the corresponding specification could provide a basis for a development of a computer code for creation of prototype data from measured ones. The basic request is that prototype data should represent approximately the same information about the phenomenon as the measured ones, but should be less numerous.

It is known that human intelligence is related to formation of notions that are utilized in thought processes. The notions are primarily formed by a self-organized interaction of neurons in the brain based on excitation by very complex signals generated by a network of sensors and in fact represent our perceptions in a kind of compressed thought representation of the world. We therefore expect that methods developed in the field of artificial intelligence in relation to self-organized memory formation could lead us to an efficient compression of overwhelming data to acceptable prototype ones (Grabec et al., 1997; Grabec, 1990; Kohonen, 1989). For this purpose we utilize recently developed methods of experimental statistical modeling of physical laws (Grabec et al., 1997; Grabec, 2001, 2005).

In the next chapter we explain the fundamentals of this modeling, which leads us to the formulation of the generalized Gaussian mixture model and its cost function that is applicable for quantitative description of model characteristics.

The adaptation of the model to measured data that follows from the analysis of the cost function finally leads us to a specification of a proper set of representative data. For this purpose a new algorithm is proposed and applied to the formulation of a proper model of experimentally observed phenomenon in terms of representative data. Its performance is demonstrated on data generated by a deterministic chaotic process as well as recorded traffic data.

2. Fundamentals

In order to explain the fundamentals of statistical modeling of physical laws we first consider a one-dimensional stochastic phenomenon characterized by N measurements of variable x using an instrument with span $S_x = (-L, L)$, while a generalization to a multi-dimensional case is straightforward and will be explained later. We assume that the accuracy of measurement is specified by the calibration of the instrument on a unit u. The probability density function (PDF) of the instrument output distribution during calibration is described by the scattering function $g(x, \bar{x}, \sigma)$. The mean value $\bar{x}$ and the standard deviation σ can be determined statistically by a calibration performed on the instrument using the unit u. When the scattering is caused by mutually independent disturbances in the instrument, the scattering function is described by the Gaussian PDF (Grabec et al., 1997; Lesurf, 2002):

$$g(x, \bar{x}, \sigma) = \frac{1}{\sqrt{2\pi}\sigma} \exp\left[\frac{-(x-\bar{x})^2}{2\sigma^2}\right]. \tag{1}$$

Without essential loss of generality we assume that standard deviation σ is a constant and apply such function in our further treatment. In addition to the scattering function we introduce also a uniform reference PDF: $\rho(x) = 1/(2L)$ indicating that all outcomes of the experiment are hypothetically equally probable before performing an experiment.

Let x_i denote the most probable instrument output in the n-th experiment. Using $g(x, x_n, \sigma)$ we describe the properties of the explored phenomenon during the n-th experiment. Similarly, the properties in a series of N repeated experiments, that yield the basic statistical set of experimental samples: $(x_n; n = 1, \ldots, N)$, are described by the experimental PDF over the kernel estimator:

$$f_e(x) = \sum_{n=1}^{N} p_n \, g(x, x_n, \sigma) \tag{2}$$

in which p_n denotes the probability assigned to the n-th sample. Since all experimental samples are equivalent their probabilities are equal: $p_n = 1/N$.

Properties of this estimator have been widely examined elsewhere (Parzen, 1962; Fukunaga, 1972; Duda et al., 1973; Révésh, 1991; Grabec et al., 1997; Grabec, 2001, 2005) and could be summarized as follows. With an increasing number of experimental samples N, the PDF estimated by Eq. (2) converges to a hypothetical one, and consequently, the kernel estimator Eq. (2) resembles a consistent estimator. Although it is biased, the bias can be diminished if the accuracy of experimental observation is improved by decreasing the standard deviation σ. Hence, the kernel estimator appears to represent an acceptable basis for experimental estimation of PDF. However, a deficiency is that the formulation of the kernel estimator does not include a specification of a proper number of experimental data, and consequently, we try to improve it by the definition of a generalized Gaussian mixture model (Fukunaga, 1972; Duda et al., 1973; Révésh, 1991; Grabec et al., 1997; MM).

3. Gaussian Mixture Model and Representative Data

During experimental acquisition of data it is usually observed that initial data points are on average well separated. In this case the scattering functions in the sum of Eq. (2) are not overlapping and it seems reasonable to keep them in the PDF estimator. However, at very large number of data N, a new datum on average falls into close vicinity of some previously acquired one which results in the overlapping of scattering functions, and consequently, it seems redundant to include a new term into the estimator. A particular experimental data sample contributes to the empirically estimated PDF at the sample point an amount that is proportional to its probability $p = 1/N$. This further means that overlapping caused by increasing N results in an ever finer adaptation of the experimentally estimated PDF to the hypothetical one. However, an equivalent effect can be achieved by just adapting the probability weight p of already existing data instead of increasing the number of terms in the estimator. This reasoning leads us to a slight generalization of the PDF estimator by changing Eq. (2) to the equation of Gaussian mixture model:

$$f_r(x) = \sum_{m=1}^{M} p_m \, g(x, q_m, \sigma) \tag{3}$$

Here the couple p_m, q_m denotes the probability p_m and the center q_m of the m-th representative prototype datum. $M \leq N$prototypes represent the parameters of the PDF model in Eq. (3), however an essential difference with respect to the experimentally determined estimator given in Eq. (2) is that probabilities of representative data p_m need not be equal. To simplify our expressions we further use for the model basis functions the notation: $g(x, q_m, \sigma) = g_m(x)$. Eq. (3) coincides with Eq. (2) if we put: $q_n = x_n$, $p_n = 1/N$, $M = N$. Therefore, various statistics introduced for the characterization of PDF modelling are applicable in both cases and we omit in their definitions the index that describes experimental or representative PDF.

With the introduction of the mixture model, there appears a question how we could judiciously determine a proper set of its parameters. At the first glance the problem could be classified as the adaptation of a parametric model to some hypothetical PDF: $f_h(x)$. But this is in fact much more involved since we do not know in advance neither the number of parameters nor their values $(p_m, q_m; m = 1, ..., M)$. In addition, we also do not know exactly the hypothetical PDF, but just its empirical estimator given by Eq. (2). So a proper strategy for the solution of this problem has to be found. For this purpose we apply the model information defined in previous articles (Grabec, 2001, 2005, 2009a,b). It stems from the indeterminacy of the modeled phenomenon described by the negative value of the relative entropy of PDF $f(x)$:

$$H = -\int_{S_x} f(x) \log \left[\frac{f(x)}{\rho(x)} \right] dx \; . \tag{4}$$

Similarly we define the indeterminacy of scattering functions $g_m(x)$ by means over the model probabilities p_m:

$$H_b = -\int_{S_x} \sum_{m=1}^{M} p_m \, g_m(x) \log \frac{g_m(x)}{\rho(x)} \, dx \tag{5}$$

By the difference between the indeterminacy of model and scattering functions we define the information contained in the model:

$$I = H - H_b \ . \tag{6}$$

In agreement with this definition we apply here for all information statistics the unit *nat*. The maximal possible value of information is $I_{\max} = \log(M)$. It is observed when prototype data are mutually separated for much more than standard deviation σ. However, this is generally not the case, and consequently, the information contained in the model is usually less than the maximal possible value: $I < I_{\max}$. The remaining value $I_{\max} - I$ in a sense describes the information lost in the experimental observation and indicates how much the experimental observation is redundant. Therefore, we introduce it as an additional variable called redundancy (Grabec, 2001):

$$R = \log M - I \ . \tag{7}$$

Since the statistics I, R represent the amount of information contained and missing in the model, we define its information cost function by the difference (Grabec, 2001):

$$C = R - I = \log M - 2I \ . \tag{8}$$

In order to describe how well the mixture model represents the properties of the experimentally determined PDF, we describe their discrepancy (i.e., the estimation error) by the Kullback-Leibner divergence (Grabec et al., 1997; Cover et al., 1991; Kolmogorov, 1956; MacKay, 2003):

$$D_{re} = \int_{S_x} [f_r(x) - f_e(x)] \log \frac{f_r(x)}{f_e(x)} dx \ . \tag{9}$$

In the case when a hypothetical PDF $f_h(x)$ is given we can use this equation to describe the divergence between $f_h(x)$ and $f_r(x)$ as well.

Our final goal is to adapt the prototype data to experimental samples and to characterize this process quantitatively by an information statistic. For this purpose we define the relative cost of representative model with respect to the experimental one as:

$$C_{re} = D_{re} + C_r - C_e \tag{10}$$

In the case when the model PDF closely fits the experimental one, their divergence is negligible: $D_{re} \approx 0$ and information contents approximately equal: $I_r \approx I_e$. In this case the relative cost function is approximately determined by the difference of corresponding redundancies: $C_{re} \approx R_r - R_e$. The main goal of the representative model formation should thus be first to create a proper number of prototype data that approximately describe the properties of experimental PDF and next to adapt them so that the divergence is further diminished. In this case both PDFs are approximately equal while experimental data are properly compressed to prototype ones.

4. Adaptation of the Mixture Model to Experimental Data

If we want to adapt the model described by Eq. (3) to the given PDF $f_e(x)$ we have to determine the number M and values of parameters $(p_m, q_m; m = 1,..., M)$ so that the minimum of the model cost function C_{re} is achieved. We cannot perform this by a standard variation method since M is an integer number (Grabec et al., 1997). Even if we know the number M, equations derived by variation of the cost function are non-linear and cannot be solved generally. Consequently, we do not consider the general problem anymore, but rather, turn to the problem of model adaptation to an increasing number of experimental data samples. Various approximate methods of growing and pruning have been proposed for this purpose in the field of neural networks (Haykin, 1999; Leonardis et al., 1998). The growing methods are mainly utilized when the model is adapted to an increasing number of experimental samples, while pruning is used when a numerous set of experimental samples is compressed to a less numerous set of representative data. Since we do not want to store overwhelming data we next consider just the case with the increasing number of experimental samples. In the literature various criteria have already been proposed for this purpose, but at present there is still no generally accepted method. Consequently, we here propose an acceptable method that is based upon rather intuitive concepts stemming from the interpretation of experimental data.

At the adaptation of the representative model to an increasing number of experimental samples we have to consider a proper creation as well as adaptation of prototype data. In order to proceed to a proper strategy for the solution of this problem let us consider the case when $f_r(x) \approx f_e(x)$ and examine what happens when the number of experimental data values is increased from N to $N+1$. In this case the experimental PDF $f_{e,N}(x)$ is changed to $f_{e,N+1}(x)$. The corresponding difference is:

$$\Delta f_e(x) = f_{e,N+1}(x) - f_{e,N}(x) = \frac{1}{N+1} g_{N+1}(x) - \frac{1}{N+1} f_{e,N}(x). \qquad (11)$$

The first term represents a localized contribution of the $N+1^{st}$ data sample, while the second one represents the decrease of the complete PDF in order to preserve its normalization. Since $f_r(x) \approx f_{e,N}(x)$ we can most simply adapt the model to the last term of Eq. (10) by multiplying all probabilities $p_m; m=1,...,M$ by the factor $1-1/(N+1) = N/(N+1)$. Less direct is adaptation to the first term on the right side of Eq. (11). For this purpose we assume that all experimental samples which fall into the typical interval of instrumental scattering $(q-\sigma, q+\sigma)$ in fact denote the same experimental result as the central value q and then consider two characteristic situations:

I. The experimental sample x_{N+1} takes place near some closest prototype q_c so that $|q_c - x_{N+1}| \le \sigma$. In this case we achieve a proper adaptation by joining the new sample x_{N+1} with the prototype q_c. At this step the probability of prototype is increased: $p_c \to p_c + 1/(N+1)$ and its center is moved to the center of gravity of the new sample x_{N+1} and prototype q_c:

$$q_c \to \frac{q_c p_c + x_{N+1}/(N+1)}{p_c + 1/(N+1)}. \qquad (12)$$

As the weights for calculation of center of gravity of the experimental sample and prototype center we use the probabilities appertaining to them.

II. The data sample x_{N+1} is not close to any prototype so that $|q_m - x_{N+1}| > \sigma$ for all *m*. In this case we achieve a proper adaptation by creating a new prototype having the center at the sample value: $q_{M+1} = x_{N+1}$ and the probability: $p_{M+1} = 1/(N+1)$.

If we follow these steps we obtain prototype parameters (p_m, q_m) that represent mean values of experimental samples in the scattering interval around them and carrying their probabilities. By numerical investigations of various characteristic examples we have found, that the resulting prototype samples are mutually spaced for approximately 1.5σ. Treatment described by steps I and II yields at an increasing number of experimental samples N ever better adapted representative model, although the number of prototypes is generally stabilized (Grabec, 2009a,b). Since the PDFs are then approximately equal: $f_r(x) \approx f_e(x)$, the corresponding information is also approximately equal: $I_r(x) \approx I_e(x)$, while the divergence is small $D_{re} \approx 0$. However, the redundancy of experimental model is increasing as: $R_e(x) \approx \log N$, while the redundancy of the representative model converges to some fixed value: $R_r(x) \approx \log M \approx \text{const.}$ Therefore, the adaptation of prototypes at an increasing number of experimental samples N yields decreasing relative cost: $C_{re} \approx \text{const.} - R_e$. One could then expect that it is needed to increase the number of experimental samples without limit to find a proper representative model. However this is not the case since the number of prototypes M stops increasing at some characteristic value $M_{\max}$ indicating that the representative model is properly formed. In tune with this property it seems reasonable to stop acquisition of experimental samples when the number of prototypes M stops increasing. In such a case we say that the prototypes properly represent the information provided by the experimental observation. At the corresponding number of experimental samples the relative cost C_{re} is then minimal, and consequently we can assume that the corresponding Gaussian mixture model optimally represents the experimental one.

The adaptation steps described in I and II can be simply transformed into a computer code. A transition from the first to the second step occurs when the distance between a new sample and the closest representative prototype surpasses the width σ of the scattering function. The resulting procedure starts by equalizing the first data sample with the first prototype: $x_1 = q_1$ and yields a proper model when the number of prototype samples stops increasing. If there is given an overwhelming set of experimental data samples, the corresponding scattering functions in the experimental estimator of PDF Eq. (2) exhibit expressive overlapping which corresponds to a high information cost. In such a case we find that the corresponding proper model is comprised of essentially less representative data with scattering functions just slightly overlapping, while the resulting PDF estimator approximately corresponds to the hypothetical PDF. The proposed method thus represents an efficient compression of data without essential loss of information.

At the application of the proposed algorithm there appears a problem when the width σ of the scattering function is not given. In such a case the value of σ could be specified by the user and with respect to the wanted accuracy of PDF modeling. Quite generally one can suggest normalizing the variable x with respect to its variance. This yields a relative variable: $r = x / \sqrt{\mathrm{var}(x)}$. Specification of σ_r corresponding to this variable then determines how detailed is the modeling of the PDF. Such a treatment also renders possible comparison of various models.

The next problem appears when the phenomenon is characterized by a multi-dimensional vector variable $\mathbf{x} = (x_1, x_2, ..., x_d)$. In this case the scattering function can be first described by the multi-dimensional Gaussian distribution while all previously defined statistics can be generalized by corresponding changing of the integral in the specification of the information entropy. In addition, it is often convenient to normalize the i-th component separately with respect to its variance: $r_i = x_i / \sqrt{\mathrm{var}(x_i)}$. If the components represent similar properties of the phenomenon, then some common average σ can be applied as a relative measure for the description of the level separating the steps I and II of the method. In our subsequent example of traffic flow modeling we apply this method.

In relation to the formulation of the mixture model given in Eq. (3) one could expect that there is possible still further generalization by adapting also the width of scattering functions corresponding to different prototypes in the representative model: $\sigma \rightarrow \sigma_m$. Although such a generalization could yield still more compressed model (Grabec, 2001; Kohonen, 1989), the interpretation of generalized model basis functions in terms of scattering functions is lost, and therefore a representative datum cannot be interpreted as a typical result of measurement. Consequently, we do not proceed here with such a generalization.

5. Examples of Compression

5.1. Compression of Two Samples

To demonstrate some basic properties of the formulated algorithm we first consider a simple example when two equally probable experimental samples are compressed to a single prototype. For the sake of simplicity we select the width$\sigma = 1$ and analyze changing of statistics$f_e, f_r, I_e, R_e, C_e, C_r, I_{re}, C_{re}$when the spacing of samples increases.

Figure 1 shows the corresponding PDFs for the following discrete set of spacing: $x_2 - x_1 = 0{,}2{,}3{,}4{,}5{,}6$. The dependence of statisticsf_e, f_r on the spacing$x_2 - x_1$ in the continuous interval (0,6) is shown in Figure 2.

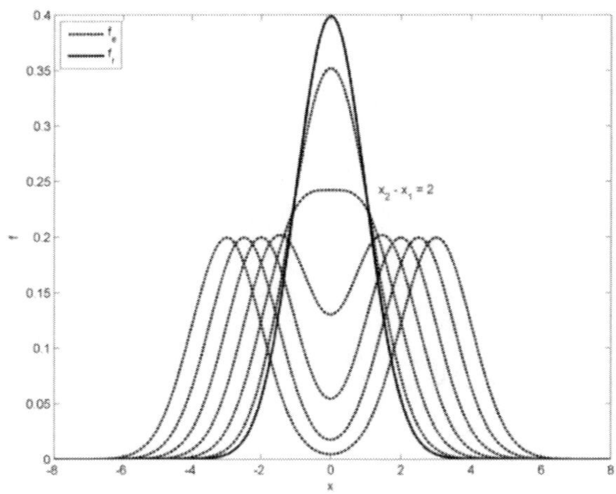

Figure 1. Experimental probability density function $f_e(x)$ (--) corresponding to different spacing of samples: $x_2 - x_1 = 0{,}1{,}2{,}3{,}4{,}5{,}6$ and the representative PDF $f_r(x)$ (-) determined by the compressed prototype: $q = 0, p = 1$.

In all cases just one prototype with the probability$p_1 = 1$ takes place at$q_1 = 0$ and determines the representative PDF that coincides with the scattering function:$f_r = g(\mathrm{x}, 0)$ shown in the middle of the figure.

At large separation of experimental samples the appertaining scattering functions just slightly overlap, and consequently, the information is approximately equal to: $I_e \approx \log 2$. Therefore, the redundancy vanishes:

$R_e \approx 0$ and the cost function is: $C_e \approx -\log 2$. With a decreasing spacing: $x_2 - x_1 \to 0$ the information is decreasing: $I_e \to 0$ and redundancy increasing: $R_e \to \log 2$, so that the cost function approaches to: $C_e \approx \log 2$ The value of the cost function vanishes: $C_e = 0$ at $x_2 - x_1 = 2\sigma = 2$.

At small spacing the difference between f_e and f_r is not expressive, and consequently, the divergence is small: $D_{re} \approx 0$, but with the increasing spacing the difference becomes ever more pronounced and leads to increasing value of divergence. This property is shown in Figure 3.

The fact that the information cost function C_e changes sign at the spacing $x_2 - x_1 = 2$ indicates that it is not reasonable to apply both samples when spacing between them is small, but rather to compress them to just one prototype. However, when deciding about that we have to take into account also the difference between experimental and representative PDF that is described in terms of information entropy by the divergence D_{re}.Its dependence on the spacing of samples is shown in Figure 3.

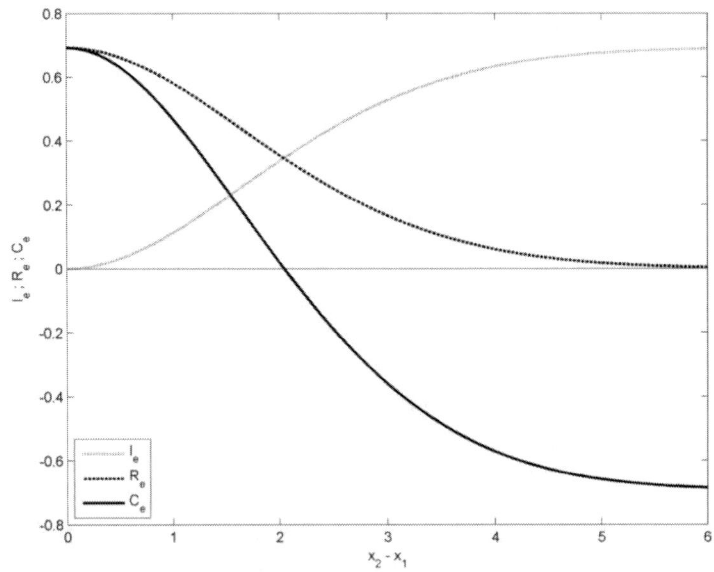

Figure 2. Dependence of information statistics I_e, R_e, C_e on the spacing $x_2 - x_1$.

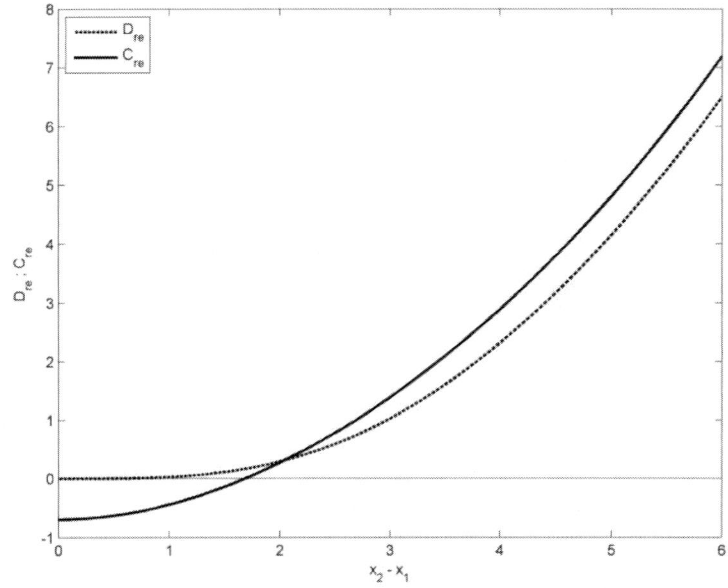

Figure 3. Dependence of the divergence D_{re} and the relative cost function C_{re} on the spacing $x_2 - x_1$.

Since it is increasing with the increasing spacing we rather take into account the properties of relative cost function C_{re} when characterizing the effect of compression. The dependence of the relative cost function C_{re} on the spacing $x_2 - x_1$ between samples is also shown in Figure 3. It indicates that compression is reasonable for spacing in the interval (0, 1.75).

This result refers to the present simple example with two equally probable samples and cannot be simply generalized to examples with many samples. Numerical investigation of examples with samples of essentially different probabilities indicates that compression can be justified also at much larger spacing. For instance, if $p_1 = 0.9$ and $p_2 = 0.1$ the corresponding interval is approximately (0, 3).

In tune with this, we can expect that compression of experimental data that are spaced for less than approximately 1.75 width of scattering function would quite generally diminish relative information cost C_{re}.

5.2. Compression of Chaotic Data

To demonstrate the performance of our method more in details we consider next the compression of chaotic data, generated by the logistic map: $y_{n+1} = 3.8\, y_n(1 - y_n)$ and transformed to the span $S_x = (-10,10)$ by the formula: $x_n = 20\ (y_n - 0.5)$. To simulate an experiment we assume that sample values are measured by an instrument having the scattering width $\sigma = 0.5$. The hypothetical PDF $f_h(x)$ of the corresponding phenomenon is estimated by the kernel estimator Eq. (2) and $N_h = 10^4$ samples.

The result is shown in Figure 4 by the line (...) together with the PDF of the experimental and representative model: $f_e(x)$, $f_r(x)$ calculated from $N = 10^3$ samples. A good agreement between experimental and representative PDF is obvious. Both functions differ slightly from the hypothetical one due to much smaller number of samples used in their estimation.

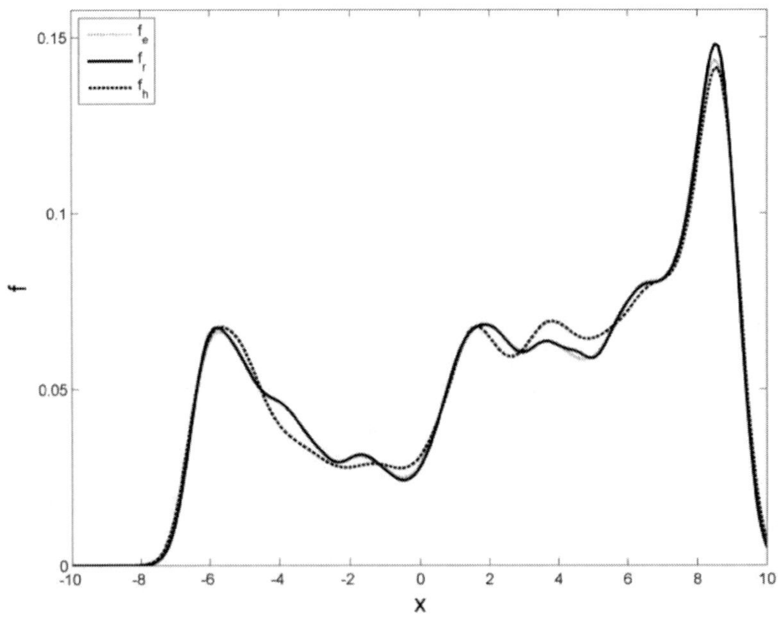

Figure 4. Probability density functions of chaotic phenomenon. $f_e(x)$ and $f_r(x)$ are determined from 10^3 samples while $f_h(x)$ is estimated from 10^4 samples.

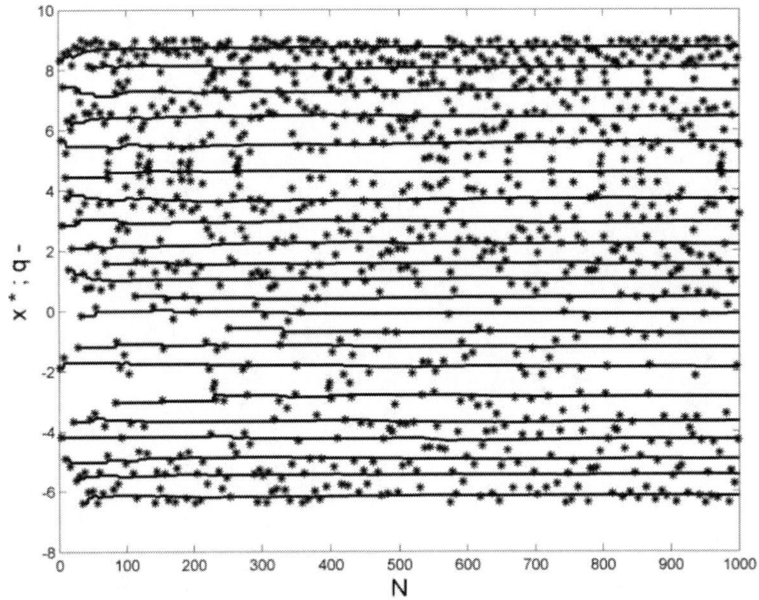

Figure 5. Formation of prototypes at the increasing number N of experimental samples. Acquisition of experimental samples x_n is denoted by points (*) while creation and adaptation of a prototypes q_n is denoted by solid lines (-).

Formation of prototypes with increasing number of experimental samples N is graphically demonstrated in Figure 5. Acquisition of experimental samples is denoted by points (*) while creation and adaptation of prototypes is denoted by solid lines (-). The prototypes are mainly created by the step I of the algorithm during acquisition of approximately 200 initial experimental samples, while later on they are slightly adapted to samples by the step II. The first property is still better demonstrated by Figure 6 that shows the dependence of prototype number on the number of samples: $M(N)$. It is evident that approximately $M \approx 22$ prototypes properly represent the properties of chaotic data PDF at the selected accuracy of observation. After the formation of the representative model the prototypes are spaced for approximately 1.5σ.The distribution of probability p_k over prototypes q_k is shown in Figure 7 and resembles the distribution of PDF.

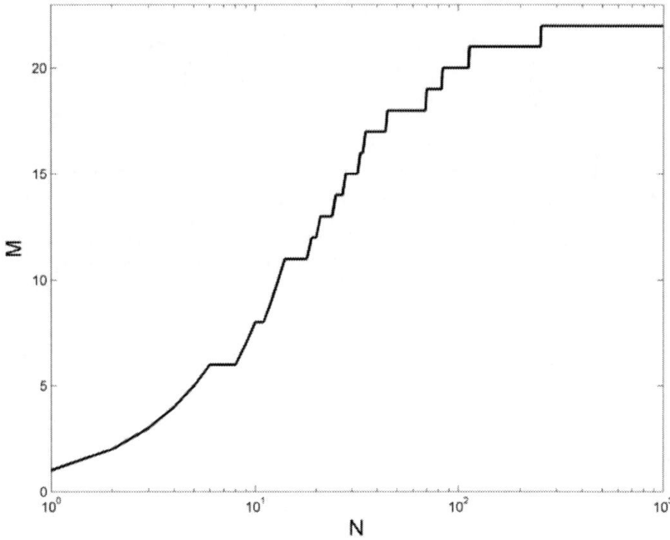

Figure 6. Dependence of the prototype number M on the number of samples N .

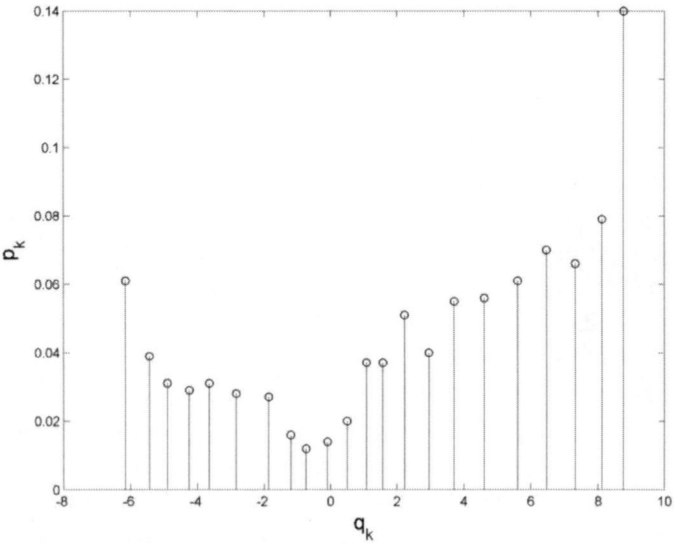

Figure 7. Distribution of probability p_k over prototypes q_k .

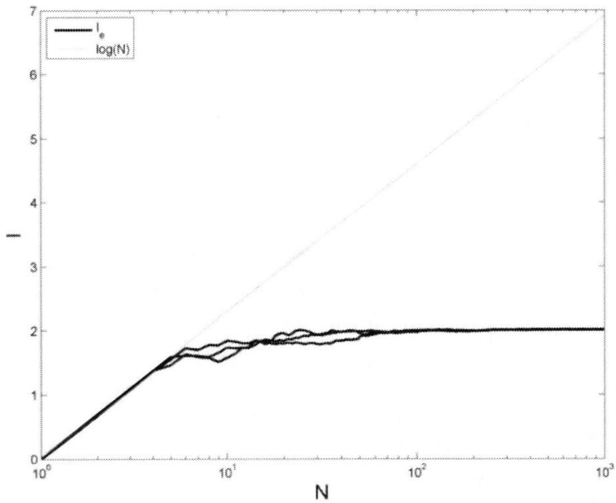

Figure 8. Dependence of the experimental information I_e on the number N estimated from three different sets of samples. The straight line denotes the maximal possible value of information given by $\log(N)$.

With the acquisition of samples the experimental information I_e first increases similarly as $\log(N)$ and then converges to a fixed value as shown by Figure 8. From the graph of $I_e(N)$ we can conclude that about 10 samples are already sufficient to roughly estimate the information provided by experimental observation in the treated example. In the initial phase of data acquisition the values of I_e estimated from different sets of samples slightly differ due to statistical fluctuations, but at approximately 200 samples I_e statistical fluctuations vanish and the value of I_e becomes fixed. This property indicates that the formation of the empirical model is practically completed.

As shown by Figure 9 the vanishing of information growth with the increasing number of samples N is accompanied by the growth of redundancy R_e that resembles the growth of $\log(N)$. However, the growth of the representative model redundancy R_r stops at approximately 200 samples. This also indicates that the formation of the representative model is practically completed. Similar conclusions can be drawn also from the dependence of information cost functions C_e and C_r on the number of samples N that is shown in Figure 10.

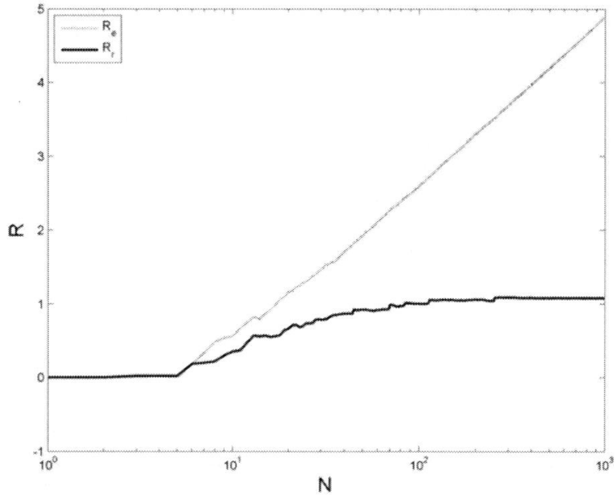

Figure 9. Dependence of redundancy R_e and R_r on the number of samples N.

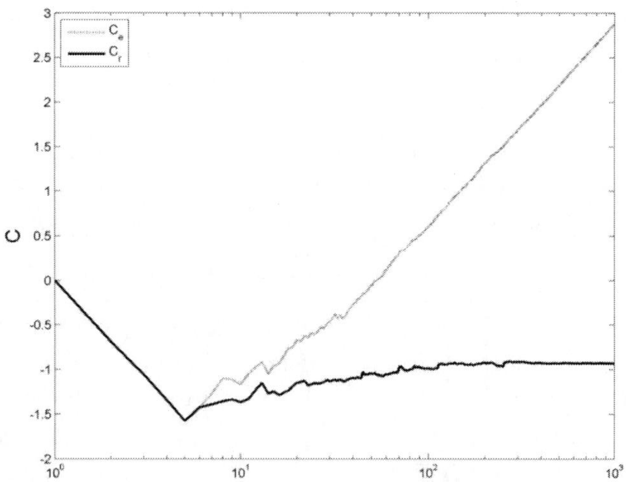

Figure 10. Dependence of the information cost functions C_e and C_r on the number of samples N.

Due to increasing information provided by the initial acquisition of data the information cost is decreasing and reaches the minimum at approximately 10 samples when the model is roughly formed. After that, the cost starts increasing due to increasing redundancy. However, changing of C_e and C_r is different, since the redundancy of the experimental model R_e is increasing while the redundancy R_r converges to a fixed value with the increasing number N of samples.From the minimum of the information cost function the number of samples needed for a proper modeling can be just roughly estimated, since the experimental information and redundancy are treated equally in the formula: $C_e = R_e - I_e$. At a low number of samples the model just roughly corresponds to the hypothetical PDF and consequently, when estimating a proper number of model terms we have to take into account also the properties of divergence shown by Figure 11.

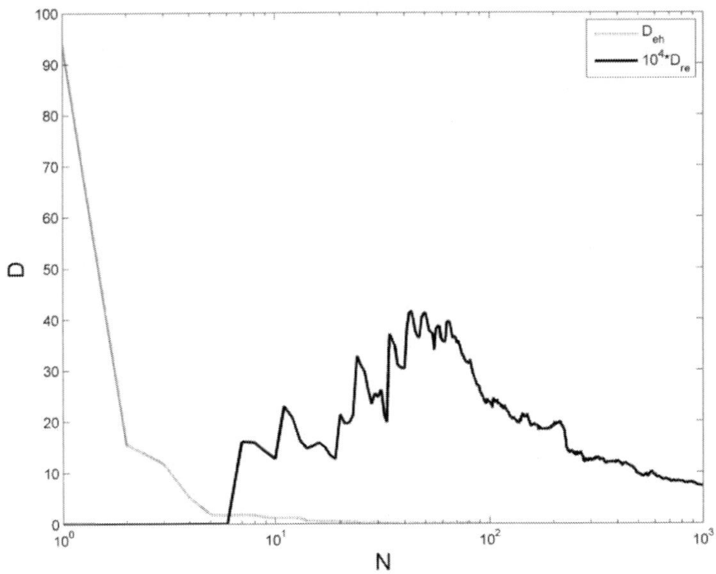

Figure 11. Dependence of divergence D_{eh} and D_{re} on the number of samples N.

In the initial phase of data acquisition the divergence between the empirical and hypothetical PDF is decreasing most expressively in the interval $1 \le N \le 10$ corresponding to the rough formation of the experimental model. In opposition to this the divergence between the representative and empirical

PDF is ~0 in the initial phase since there practically each sample is converted to a prototype. In the following phase the prototypes are less created but mainly adapted. This results first in increasing and later again decreasing divergence. However, due to good agreement between $f_e(x)$ and $f_r(x)$ the divergence D_{re} is there for about 10^4 smaller than the average D_{eh} in the initial phase of data acquisition. In accordance with the properties of divergence D_{re} and information cost functions C_e and C_r the relative cost function $C_{r/e}$, shown in Figure 12, is approximately 0 in the initial phase of the representative model formation and decreases later during its adaptation to experimental samples similarly as $-\log(N)$. The properties of statistics mentioned above are qualitatively similar if a different value of σ is selected, just their values are changed. The most outstanding is increasing of the final number of prototypes $M_{\max}$ with increasing accuracy of measurement that corresponds to decreasing instrumental scattering described by the value of σ.

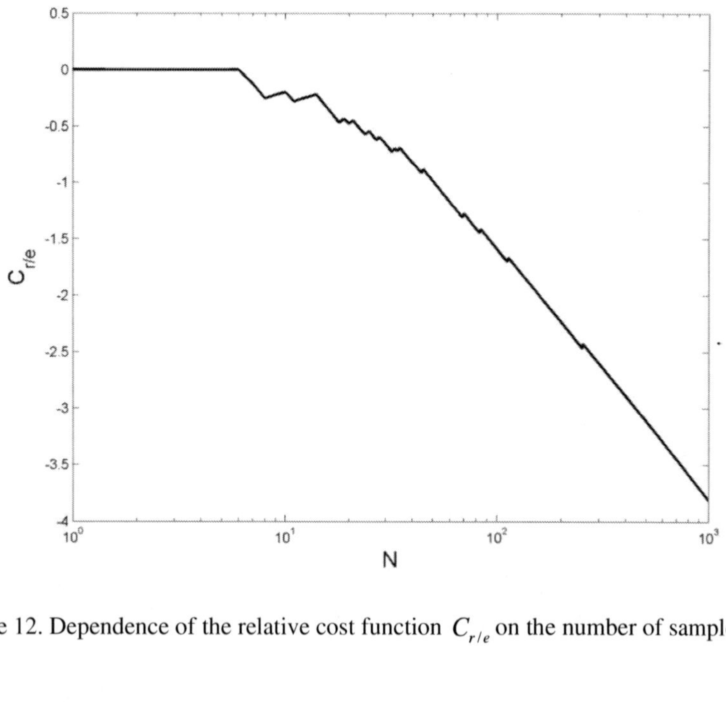

Figure 12. Dependence of the relative cost function $C_{r/e}$ on the number of samples N.

5.3. Compression of Traffic Flow Data

In order to demonstrate the applicability of the proposed compression we next consider observation of traffic flow rate on a road. As an example we utilize here data obtained at some representative point on a high-way in Slovenia (Grabec, 2010). For the sake of simplicity we consider just a single category of cars and describe the measured traffic flow rate by the variable $Q(t)$. This variable depends on time of observation t so that a measurement yields a record of corresponding time series: $\{ Q(t) ; t = 0, \Delta t, 2\Delta t, ..., T \}$. Here $\Delta t = 1\text{h}$ denotes the length of time interval between successive measurements. An example of the record spanning over one year is shown in Figure 13. Without loss of generality for the description of traffic phenomenon, we further decompose the recorded time series into a set of traffic flow rate day-vectors that are comprised of 24 data recorded over the n-th day: $\mathbf{Q}(n) = (Q_1(n), ..., Q_{24}(n))$. A set of 30 day-vectors extracted from arbitrary selected days $n = 201...231$ from the record in Figure13 is shown in Figure 14. As the index of traffic day-vector component we use the hour t of its recording.

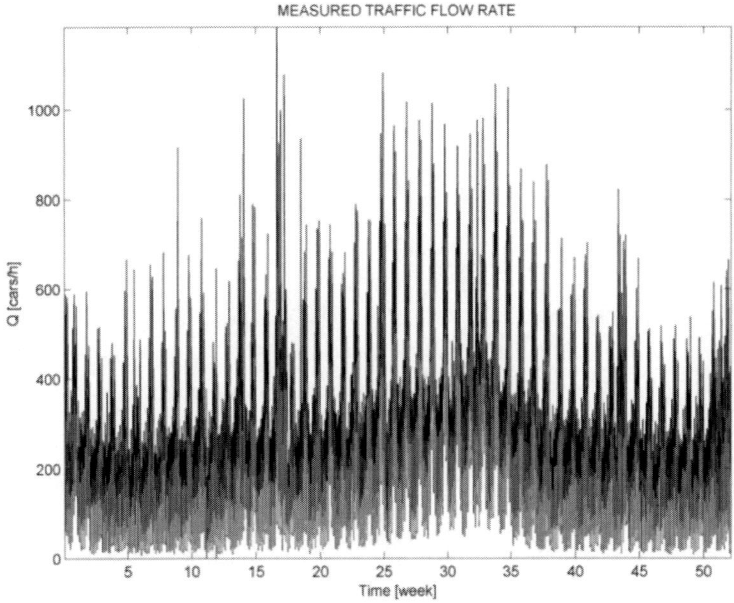

Figure 13. An example of one year long traffic flow record.

In order to proceed to the representative model we must specify some criterion for the separation of the steps I and II of the adaptation process. For this purpose we apply the variance of each day-vector component determined by the statistical mean over all days of the year.

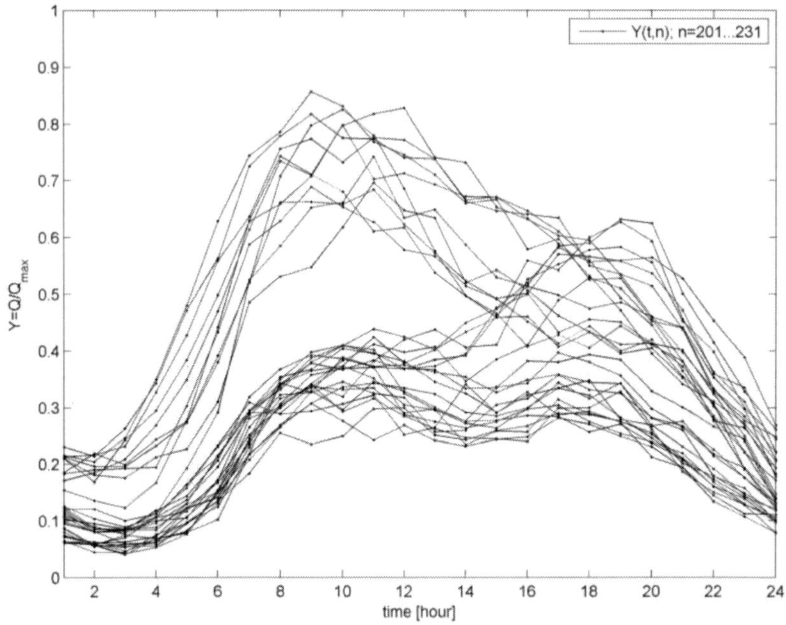

Figure 14. Normalized traffic day-vectors $Y = Q / Q_{\max}$ formed from the flow record in Figure 13 at arbitrary selected days with $n = 201...231$.

Using the corresponding variances we introduce for each component the relative distance between a given day-vector and a representative one by the formula: $d_i = (Q_i - q_i) / \sqrt{\mathrm{var}(Q_i)}$ .Using it we introduce a measure of discrepancy between the day-vector and the representative one by the mean square relative distance over a day: $\delta = \sum_{i=1}^{24} d_i^2 / 24$. As a separation level between the steps I and II we then use the value $\delta_s = 2$. This value is selected based upon numerical testing of modeling performance in which we have been looking for a characteristic level that provides for a formation of prototypes corresponding to characteristic days of the week.

Using the day-vectors and the level of separation $\delta_s = 2$ we form the representative vectors as described by steps I and II. The corresponding representative vectors are shown in Figure 15.

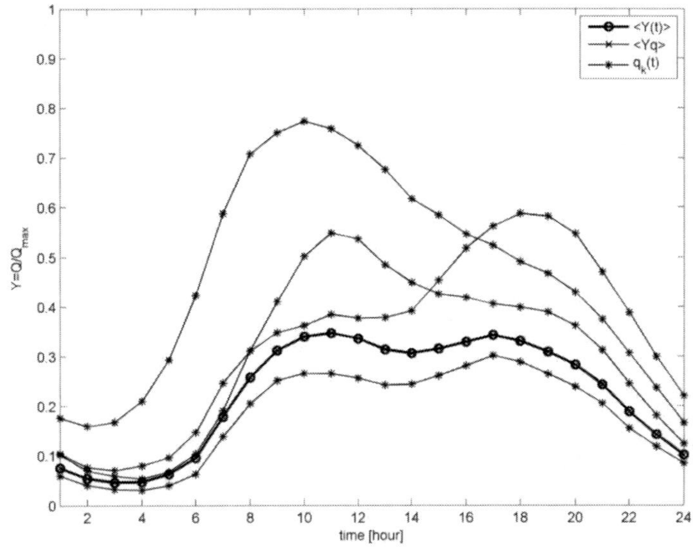

Figure 15. Representative traffic day-vectors formed from 365 measured traffic day vectors. (-o-) denotes the mean vector determined from all day-vectors and (-x-) denotes the mean vector determined from prototype vectors. Overlapping of curves (-o-) (-x-) indicates a good representation of traffic properties by the ptototypes.

In order to demonstrate applicability of representative vectors we calculate from the model PDF the mean day vector. Its record is shown in Figure 15 by the line (-x-) and coincides well with the record of the mean vector calculated directly from the complete set of day-vectors (-o-). This coincidence confirms a correct representation of traffic variable PDF by f_r.

The probabilities corresponding to representative traffic day-vectors are shown in Figure 16 in dependence of representative vector index *k*. It is interesting that 365 day-vectors from the complete year are in this case properly represented by just 4 prototype day-vectors that closely correspond to a normal day with the highest *p*, and 3 days around weekends or holidays with approximately 6 times smaller *p*. This property is evident also from Figure 17 that shows prototype traffic day-vectors in dependence of index *t* and probability *p*.

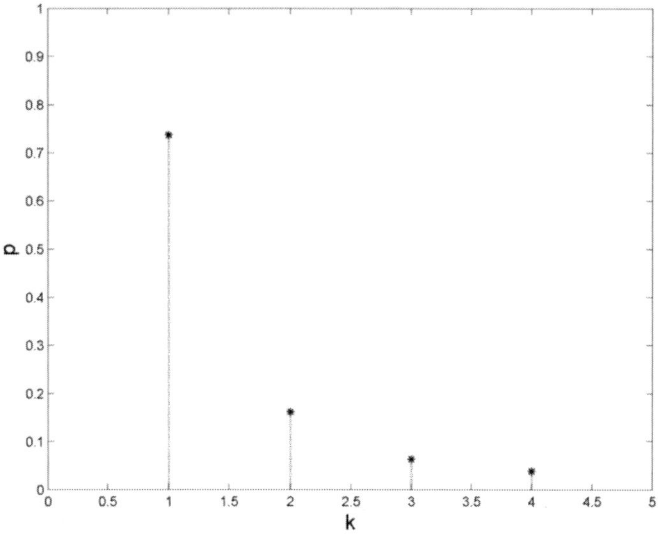

Figure 16. The distribution of probabilities corresponding to prototype traffic day-vectors formed from 365 all traffic day-vectors.

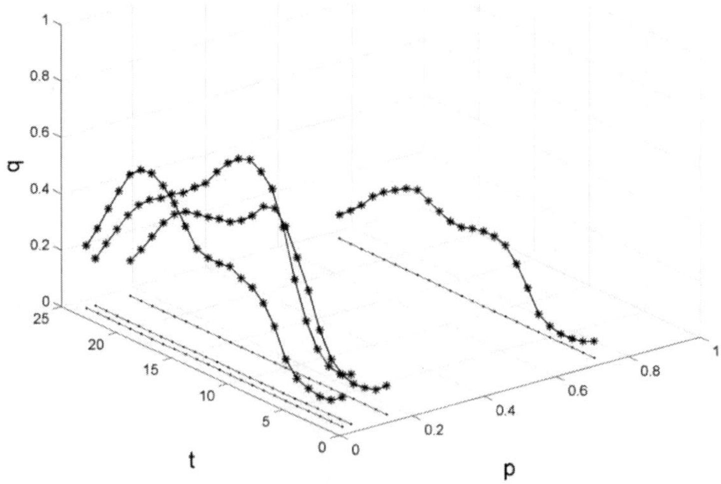

Figure 17. Presentation of prototype traffic day-vectors in dependence of index t and probability p.

Conclusion

We have shown how the PDF of a stochastic variable can be estimated by the kernel estimator and experimental data by taking into account the scattering function of the instrument. In order to avoid deficiencies of the experimental estimator we have generalized it to the Gaussian mixture model and proposed for its formation a specific algorithm. To characterize the properties of the corresponding procedure quantitatively we introduced the information, redundancy, information cost function, divergence and the relative cost function of representative model with respect to the experimental one.

With the increasing number of experimental samples the experimental PDF converges to the hypothetical one. Along with this the information of the experimental model is first increasing and then stabilized. The difference between the estimated information and the maximal possible value determined by the logarithm of the number of samples is introduced as the redundancy of data. Its value is first low but latter on increases logarithmically with the number of samples. Therefore the information cost defined by the difference of redundancy and information is first decreasing and later on increasing with the number of samples. From its minimum the number of samples needed for a rough formation of the experimental model of PDF can be estimated. Since the redundancy and the information are evenhandedly treated in the information cost function this number can be surprisingly low in comparison to the number of samples needed for a proper estimation of experimental PDF. In opposition to the redundancy of the experimental model the adaptation of the representative model to experimental data leads to a fixed redundancy and the number of prototypes although the information contained in the representative model is approximately equal to the information of the experimental model. Therefore the information cost of the representative model converges to a fixed value. Since the estimation error is vanishing due to proper adaptation of prototypes to experimental data, the relative cost function of representative model with respect to the experimental one is decreasing. From the stabilization of the number of representative samples one can estimate when a proper representative model is formed. Since the number of prototypes is quite generally much smaller than the number of experimental data required for the formation of the representative model the algorithm of the Gaussian mixture model formation corresponds to an effective and accurate compression procedure that is applicable in automatic measurement systems. As we have shown by the demonstrated example it could be of especial importance for compression of overwhelming traffic data at their storage in memory media.

The proposed adaptation represents an innovative approach to processing of complex data that could be applied also in modeling of artificial neural networks (Grabec et al., 1997; Grabec, 2013; Haykin, 1999; Leonardis et al., 1998). Adaptation of prototypes by the steps I and II is an essentially non-linear process that resembles self-organized formation of notions in thought processes of intelligent beings and can therefore substitute an intelligent operator at the archiving of traffic data.

References

Cover, T. M.; Thomas, J. A. *Elements of Information Theory*; John Wiley & Sons, New York, 1991.

Duda, R. O.; Hart, P. E. *Pattern Classification and Scene Analysis*; J. Wiley and Sons, New York, 1973, Ch.4.

Fukunaga, K. *Introduction to Statistical Pattern Recognition*; Academic Press, New York, 1972, Ch. 6.

Grabec, I. *Biol. Cyber.* 1990, 63, 403-409.

Grabec, I. *Eur. Phys. J.* B 2001, 22, 129-135.

Grabec, I. *Eur. Phys. J.* B 2005, 48, 279-286.

Grabec, I. *Int. Conf. Applied Statistics,* Ribno Bled, Slovenia, 2009, Program and Abstracts, I-9.

Grabec, I. *Neural Networks*, 2013, 41, 51-58.

Grabec, I. *Non-lin. Phen. in Compl. Sys.* 2010, 13(1), 45-52 and 2011, 14(2), 177-183.

Grabec, I.; Sachse, W. *Synergetics of Measurements, Prediction, and Control*; Springer, Berlin, 1997.

Grabec, Optimal Compression of Traffic Flow Data, *Adv. inMeth. and Stat.* 2010, 7(1), 25-37.

Haykin, S. *Neural Networks: A Comprehensive Foundation*; Prentice Hall, Upper Saddle River, NY, 1999.

Kohonen, T. *Self-Organization and Associative Memory*; Springer, Berlin, 1989.

Kolmogorov, A. N. *IEEE Trans. Inf. Theory* 1956, IT-2, 102-108.

Leonardis, A.; Bischof, H. *Neural Networks* 1998, 11, 963-973.

Lesurf, J. C. G. *Information and Measurement*; Institute of Physics Publishing, Bristol, 2002.

MacKay, D. J. C. *Information Theory*, Inference, and Learning Algorithms; Cambridge University Press, Cambridge, UK, 2003.

MM: http://en.wikipedia.org/wiki/Mixture_Model

Parzen, E. *Ann. Math. Stat*. 1962, 35, 1065-1076.

Révész, P. In *Handbook of Statistics; Krishnaiah*, P. R.; Sen, P. K; North Holland, Amsterdam, 1991, Vol. 4, pp 531-549.

Treiber, M.; Kesting, A. *Traffic flow Dynamics, Data, Models and Simulation*; Springer, Berlin, 2013.

In: Network Coding and Data Compression
Editor: MaryAnn Simmons
ISBN: 978-1-63483-185-7
© 2015 Nova Science Publishers, Inc.

Chapter 6

CASCADE SCHEME OF DATA COMPRESSION IN MULTIMODE FIBER SYSTEMS

D. V. Svistunov[*]
St. Petersburg State Polytechnic University,
St. Petersburg, Russia

Abstract

Cooperative application of different data compression methods is an evident way to build advanced fiber systems with high information capacity. Intensive investigations resulted in development of the techniques that form the groups of time division multiplexing (TDM) and wavelength division multiplexing (WDM) methods. Furthermore, progress in fiber manufacturing technology enables fabricating multimode fibers demonstrating enhanced performances that allow using another data compression method – mode division multiplexing (MDM). Therefore, three-level hierarchic scheme of data compression in multimode fiber systems can be composed. The use of the techniques of TDM method is the content of the first stage. At the second stage, compressed information channels must be combined by WDM techniques. And the MDM technique should be applied at the highest hierarchic stage providing independent transmission of obtained complex information channels over the same multimode fiber. Combination of TDM and WDM techniques is realizable in practice, whereas application of MDM technique at the third stage depends on performances of the units providing selective mode excitation in multimode fibers. Results of experimental study of the developed selective waveguide element which could demonstrate

[*] E-mail address: svistunov@mail.ru.

perceptible spectral sensitivity show that this element is capable of providing cooperative application of WDM and MDM techniques. Hence these results prove realizability of three-stage cascade scheme. Important advantageous feature of the cascade scheme is additional enhancement of data security in the system due to application of MDM technique.

The growth of information traffic is a steady trend in optical fiber communication. This demand should be considered when building new systems or reconstructing the existing ones. Apparent way to increase system information capacity is cooperative application of different data compression techniques in advanced systems. By the performed functions, various techniques can be combined in several groups.

The first group – time division multiplexing (TDM) method bases on managing the alternative switching of different input signal streams in turn toward the same output. In this method time domains (frames) are defined, and each one is divided into several time slots which are filled with the data blocks of transmitted signal streams. TDM method had been developed a time ago and implemented in wire and radio communications, and also in optical fiber communication on appearance of fiber systems. While two former applications use managing the electric signals (ETDM), the latter application have led to development of extra techniques performing switching of optical signal streams (OTDM). Whereas a number of variants of TDM method have been developed, further works on TDM techniques and algorithms are still performed actively.

Other groups – wavelength division multiplexing (WDM) and mode division multiplexing (MDM) are specific optical methods of data compression in optical communications. Their implementation was performed gradually as improvement of fabrication technology and performances of fibers and system units were achieved.

WDM method uses the solitary optical fiber for parallel transmission of a number of light streams of different wavelengths where each one serves as an independent information channel. Performed standardization resulted in defining several wavelength windows and also wavelength channel spacing into the window. Maximal system information capacity can be reached under employment of dense WDM (DWDM) technique capable of providing minimal channel spacing defined by the standardized spectral grid for 12.5 GHz and 25 GHz separations. At present WDM techniques have wide application in current fiber systems and are successfully used as individually as in combinations with ETDM or OTDM techniques (e.g., [1 – 3]).

The content of MDM technique is utilization of different mode groups of the same multimode fiber as independent information channels. Implementation of this method was delayed because of high intermodal coupling in former commercial fibers. However, progress in fabrication technology reduced drastically the level of intermodal coupling (as for example, conducted measurements of intermodal coupling coefficient indicated average level as 0.007 km^{-1} for the case of neighbour-order modes [4]). Due to that progress, propagation of sole modes has been obtained in multimode commercial fibers, and further investigations concentrated just on realization of MDM technique. By present, experimental MDM-based systems are developed demonstrating the available distances being quite sufficient for fiber systems like metropolitan or toll lines and local area networks (for example, [5 – 9]) even without involving the optical amplifiers. As feasibility of MDM systems is proven practically, the goal of the next stage is complex combination of this technique with other data compression methods.

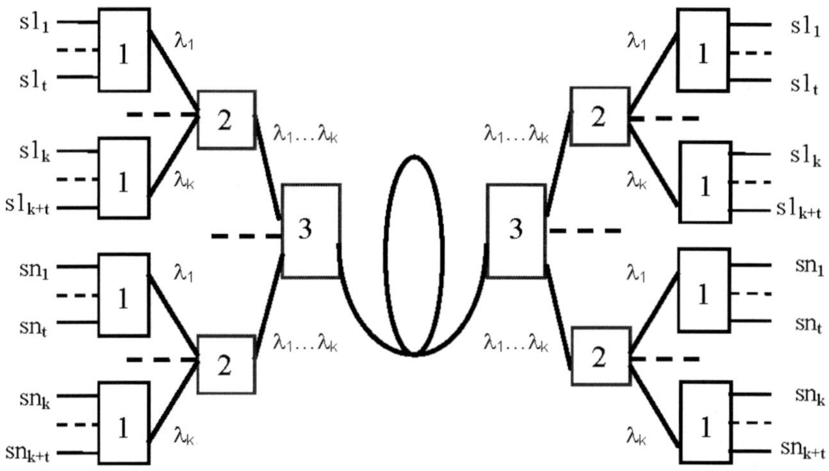

Figure 1. Hierarchical cascade scheme of data compression in multimode fiber systems. The blocks denote the devices of following types: 1 – TDM, 2 – WDM, 3 – MDM.

For this purpose, a cascade scheme that is shown in Figure 1 can be proposed. The scheme is capable of providing hierarchical three-level compression of data streams. Primary stage of data processing in the scheme bases on TDM techniques issuing the set of compressed data streams each intended for separate spectral channel. The second stage uses WDM method that joins a number of spectral channels in the same fiber. Single-mode fibers should be used in these two stages to obtain the best performances. Application of MDM technique is the content of the third stage. At this stage, each compressed optical signal resulting from previous stages launches correspondent separate mode of multimode trunk fiber. The scheme has a symmetric structure, and reverse sequence of these stages at the receiver block of the system provides recovering the initial data streams.

Every mode channel in multimode fiber can be considered as an analogue to separate single-mode fiber for which cooperative implementation of TDM and WDM techniques is already proven. So, the question concerning the proposed scheme is whether WDM and MDM techniques can be used together in practice.

Obviously, feasibility of the considered scheme depends on ability of mode multiplexers/demultiplexers to operate effectively in some spectral range. These units are based on selective mode couplers which excite/ detect independently fiber modes of different orders. A set of such elements basing on different principles have been developed (for example, [10 – 18]). In most cases selective excitation of fiber modes is performed with external units that are matched optically with the fiber by traditional or GRIN lenses, or through butt joining. The couplers based on traditional bulk optical elements demonstrate low levels of spectral sensitivity within every standard frequency range of fiber communications. However, the couplers involving fiber or integrated optical elements require special consideration. Particularly, the attention should be paid to selective units whose operating principles lead to dependence of directions of intrinsic light propagation on the light wavelength. Waveguide mode multiplexer/demultiplexer described in [19, 20] is just the unit of this kind, and experimental samples of the unit were examined to determine the noted dependence.

Scheme of the considered unit is shown in Figure 2. Planar selective element operates as a longitudinal integrated optical coupler and matches optically each mode of the multimode channel waveguide with the correspondent waveguide beam in single-mode planar region joined with the set of single-mode channel guides by horn transition structures. As planar selective coupler is the key element of the unit, experimental samples of this element have been studied by measurement of directional diagrams of planar beams [21].

Mentioned beams propagate in planar region in different directions which can be determined from the following condition of phase matching: $N_m \cdot \cos\alpha_{ij} = N_{ij}$, where N_m and N_{ij} – the mode indices of planar and channel modes accordingly, α_{ij} – the angle between planar beam axe and multimode channel guide. It must be estimated if application of certain light bandwidth could lead to superimposition of different planar beams. Reliable accurate measurement of beam directivity diagram into planar waveguide could be difficult, therefore extra prism input/ output coupler having cylindrical base was applied, and directional diagrams of output beams were measured as it is shown in Figure 3.

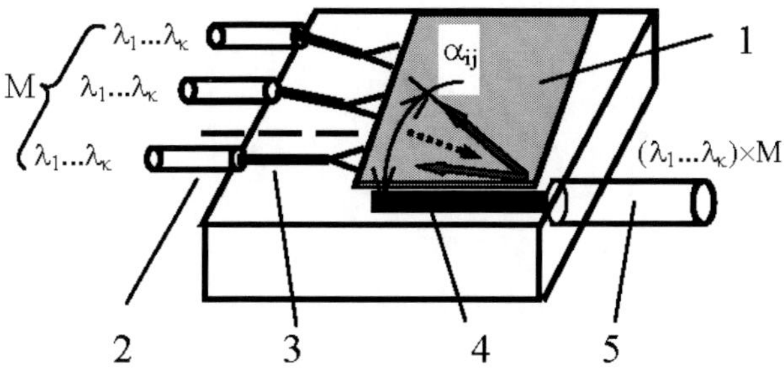

Figure 2. Scheme of waveguide unit for selective mode excitation/ detection. 1 – single-mode planar section, 2 – single-mode fibers, 3 – single-mode channel waveguides with horn transitions, 4 – multimode channel waveguide, 5 – multimode fiber.

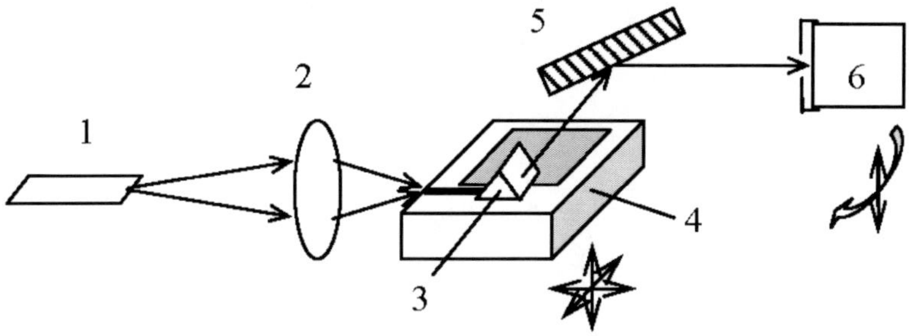

Figure 3. Examination of the unit as a mode demultiplexer. 1 – laser, 2 – focusing optical system, 3 – bulk prism coupler, 4 – examined sample, 5 – mirror, 6 – photoreceiver mounted on the goniometer alidade.

Light intensity distribution along the spatial m-line is similar to lateral power profile of the correspondent mode beam, and these distributions can be built one from another using the relation $\sin\alpha' = N_m \cdot \sin\alpha$, where α and α′ – the direction angles of light rays in planar region and output measuring plane accordingly.

Figure 4 presents the results of examinations of the trial sample. Obtained patterns are typical for all couplers of this kind. Every peak corresponds to the separate planar beam associated with the certain channel mode. The lower the mode numbers the wider the beam directional diagram.

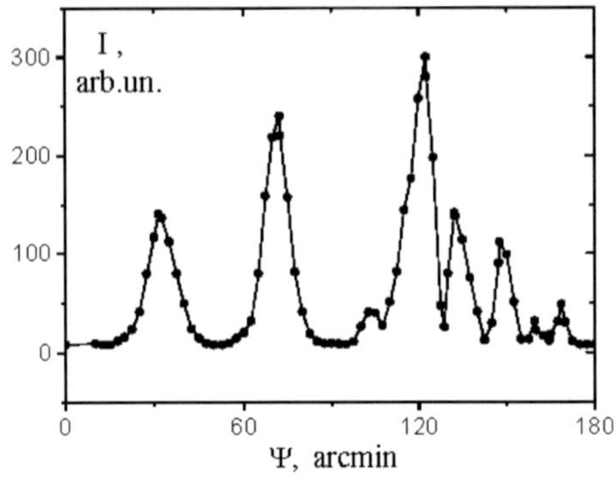

(a)

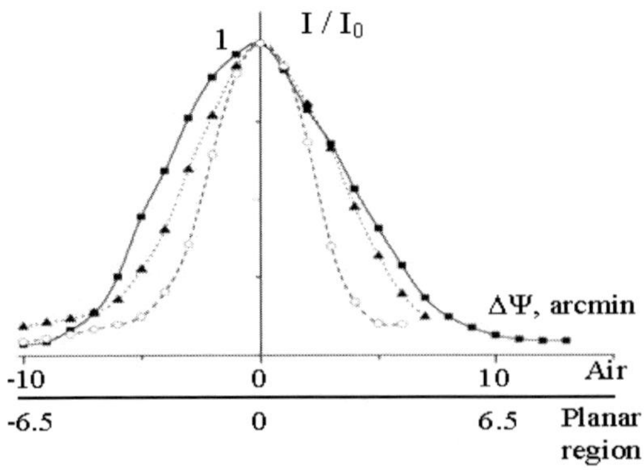

(b)

Figure 4. (a) Angular distribution of light beams associated with the set of excited channel modes. Ψ corresponds to goniometric readouts under arbitrary benchmark position. (b) Angular divergence of planar beams matched with lower-order channel modes.

Study of the sample intended for operating at light wavelength as 1.3 μm and simulation of coupler excitation with light of whole standard O bandwidth showed that angular widths of three neighbour planar beams become as 22, 20 and 16 arcmin while the angles between the axes of adjacent beams are 64 and 33 arcmin [21]. These results indicate that the beams are spatially separated and can be directed to correspondent horn structures without appearance of significant crosstalk. So, the experimental results confirm that this mode multiplexer is capable of operating with optical signals compressed by WDM. Considering that the mentioned multiplexer is assumed to be among the ones having perceptible spectral sensitivity, we can conclude that the obtained results prove feasibility of cooperative application of MDM and WDM techniques.

Advantageous feature of MDM method is opportunity to reach additional enhancement of data security in the system. Application of MDM technique allows building the systems which can issue alarm signals and/ or make difficult a procedure of illegal data reading in itself. The experimental system described in [22] can be as an example. In that system selectively excited fundamental fiber mode is exploited for high-bit-rate data transmission while several higher order modes form together the monitor channel registering illegal intrusion. When the level of monitor signal decreases, the alarm signal is issued.

However, MDM technique enables enhancing data protection even without special monitor channel. In order to prove this supposal, let us evaluate differences between mode propagation constants in commercial multimode fibers. A number of fiber systems are built on graded-index fibers having circular cross section with parabolic-like refractive index profile. Mode propagation constantsβ can be determined for these fibers as $\beta = kn_1\left[1-2(2\Delta)^{1/2}(2p+l+1)/(kn_1a)\right]^{1/2}$, where $\Delta = (n_1 - n_2)/n_1$, a – the core radius, n_1 – the maximal core index, n_2 – the cladding index, $k = 2\pi/\lambda$, λ – light wavelength in vacuum, p = 0,1,2… and l = 0,1,2… – radial and azimuthal mode numbers accordingly [23]. Defining principal mode number $M = 2p + l$as the value characterizing separate mode groups each containing the set of degenerate fiber modes, one could see equidistant dependence of the propagation constant in terms ofβ^2on the principal number M. Total amount of mode groups in the fiber is evaluated as $M_0 = kn_1a(\Delta/2)^{1/2}$ [24]. Then for adjacent groups we can write the difference $\delta(\beta^2) \approx k^2(n_1^2 - n_2^2)/M_0$. Usually in commercial fibers $\Delta \ll 1$, hence β values are close one to another for modes of adjacent numbers. It can be shown that using this condition we obtain the difference between propagation constants of neighbour modes as $\Delta\beta \approx \delta(\beta^2)/2\beta$. The value of this difference defines whether illegal data reading could be ineffective.

For further estimations we must consider typical variants of impact on the trunk fiber under illegal data reading. Illegal intrusion to the fiber system is intended to partial diversion of transmitted optical signal to some external receiver. As the character of hidden activity means non-registered intrusion, only minor part of mode power is outcoupled from the fiber. It can be done by several ways: under local bending of the fiber or with application of optical units operating as known longitudinal input/output couplers. The latter case seems more difficult in use but more dangerous with relation to the mentioned manner of data protection because longitudinal couplers can spatially separate output light beams correspondent to the modes of different orders. So we must estimate whether fiber modes can be registered separately by this manner under the specific conditions of illegal intrusion. As an example of those couplers, the prism of higher refractive index can be pressed to the trunk fiber as it is shown in Figure 5a. Phase matching condition defines the direction of the outcoupled beam: $\beta = \beta_0 \cos\gamma$, where γ – the slope angle to the fiber axis,β_0 – the propagation constant of spatial beam in higher-index medium. Determining the ratio of deviations of these values through expression for $\partial\beta / \partial\gamma$ and considering vicinity of β values in weakly guiding fiber, we can write the difference $\Delta\gamma$ between directions of outcoupled neighbour-order modes as $\Delta\gamma = \Delta\beta / (\beta_0 \sin\gamma)$. Assuming $\beta \approx k(n_1 + n_2)/2$ for some mode group of medium principal number, we obtain $\Delta\gamma \approx (2\Delta)^{1/2} / (kan_0 \sin\gamma)$ for two adjacent mode groups. Here n_0 – the refractive index of noted prism, and the condition $n_0 > n_1$ must be met. Output angle of considered medium groups can be evaluated from the matching condition as $\cos\gamma \approx (n_1 + n_2)/(2n_0)$.

As a numerical example, let us evaluate the angle between outcoupled beams associated with adjacent mode groups for commercial graded-index fiber Corning 50/125. Let us use following values: a = 25 μm, $\Delta = 0.01$, β/k = 1.486, n_0 = 1.6, λ = 1.33 μm. Calculations result in the value as $\Delta\gamma \approx$ 0.002 radians which defines the angle between beam's axes. Then we must determine beam's divergences due to diffraction. In general, light irradiation from the guide through longitudinal couplers indicates beam intensity varying along the coupling length. However, because of illegal character of data reading, there is an intention to minimize decrease of signal level at the fiber end caused by intrusion. For this purpose, weak coupling is performed, and practicable coupling lengths are much less than the one required for total light irradiation from the guide. Therefore the mode intensity varies very slightly along the treated fiber region, and we can approximate intensity with a constant value. In this case, evaluation of diffraction effect can be performed using the known model of diffraction at the gap under tilted incidence of light beam with the coupling length substituted for the gap width. Defining the coupling length as the value about 1 mm and performing mentioned evaluations we obtain that the full divergence angle is about 0.0045 radians for each beam. The obtained value exceeds the angle between beam's axes. It means that even for the used value of coupling length (rather large for meeting the conditions of hidden acting) diffraction effect does not allow separating neighbour output beams. So, the beams associated with different mode groups will overlap each other, and different information streams will be superimposed. This circumstance impedes substantially registration of single information signal and data decoding.

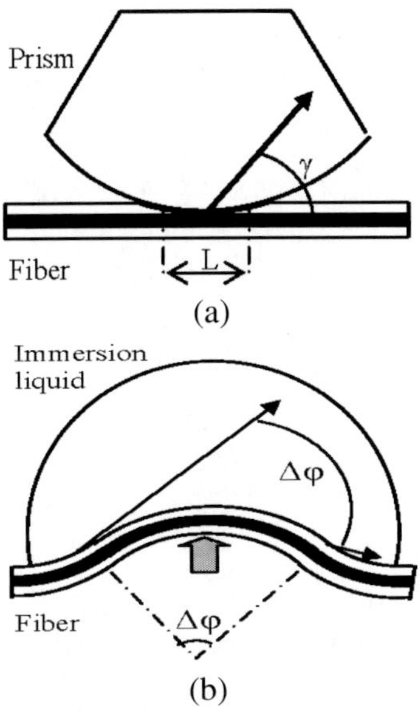

Figure 5. Possible variants of illegal intrusion: (a) using the output prism coupler, where L denotes the length of constructive coupling; (b) performing bending of the trunk fiber.

The more practical variant of illegal intrusion could use fiber bending (see Figure 5b). Because of bending, the part of the tail of mode field cross distribution is cut off and forms separate light beam (namely cladding mode) propagating into the fiber cladding. This is valid for every point along the bent fiber part, and the same cladding modes appear at every cross section of the bent fiber. Those modes can be radiated to the adjacent medium due to scattering on cladding imperfections (launching high-divergent scattered output beam) or refraction if the medium is higher-index, and also because of optical tunneling when the coupler like noted above prism is applied. As the conditions remain the same along the bend, radiated rays have equal slopes to the fiber axis at every point of bent fiber. Therefore the whole radiated beam is a high-divergent light spatial beam as one can see in Figure 5b, and the divergence angle $\Delta\varphi$ of this beam is identical with the central angle of the fiber arc formed due to external lateral pressure. It must be said that all above concern the output beam formed by one fiber mode of the certain number. Considering the noted vicinity of propagation constants of neighbour fiber modes, we can deduce obvious relation: the angle $\Delta\varphi$ is much larger than the angles between irradiated rays formed by neighbour-order modes. So, in case of fiber bending the irradiated light beams formed by different fiber modes will be superimposed totally.

Thus we can conclude that considered three-level cascade scheme of data compression in multimode fiber systems is feasible and allows tenfold increase of the system information capacity. Moreover, employment of MDM technique enables enhancing data security even without additional application of special techniques. The considered scheme can be used for building new fiber systems based on specially design few-mode fibers, and also for reconstruction of the current systems exploiting commercial multimode fibers produced last decade.

References

[1] Sivakumar, M; Subramaniam, S. *Opt Switch Netw*, 2005, 2, 100-112.

[2] Ab-bou, FM; Wong, HY; Hiew, CC; Abid, A; Chuah, HT. *J Opt Commun*, 2007, 28, 221-224.

[3] Sato, K; Hasegawa, H. *J Opt Commun Netw* 2009, 1, A81-A93.

[4] Tur, M; Menashe, D; Japha, Y; Danziger, Y. *J Opt Fib Commun Rep*, 2007, 4, 110-172.

[5] Al Amin, A; Li, A; Chen, S; Chen, X; Gao, G; Shieh, W. *Opt Expr*, 2011, 19, 16672-16678.

[6] Koebele, C; Salsi, M; Sperti, D; Tran, P; Brindel, P; Margoyan, H; Bigo, S; Boutin, A; Verluise, F; Sillard, S; Bigot-Astruc, M; Provost, L; Cerou, F; Charlet, G. *Opt Expr*, 2011, 19, 16593–16600.

[7] Ryf, R; Randel, S;Gnauck, AH; Bolle, C; Sierra, A; Mumtaz, S; Esmaeelpour, M; Burrows, EC; Essiambre, RJ; Winzer, PJ; Peckham, DW; McCurdy AH; Lingle, R Jr. *J Ligthw Technol*, 2012, 30, 521-531.
[8] Salsi, M; Koebele, C; Sperti, D; Tran, P; Mardoyan, H; Brindel, P; Bigo, S; Boutin, A;Verluise, F; Sillard, P; Bigot-Astruc, M; Provost, L; Charlet, G.*J Ligthw Technol*, 2012, 30, 618-623.
[9] Li, A; Chen, X; Al Amin, A; Ye, J; Shieh, W. *J Ligthw Technol*, 2012, 30, 3953-3964.
[10] Kawaguchi, Y; Tsutsumi, K. *Electron Lett*, 2002, 38, 1701-1702.
[11] Lee, BT; Shin, SY. *Opt Lett*, 2003, 28, 1660-1662.
[12] Karpeev, SV; Pavelyev, VS; Khonina, SN; Kazanskiy, NL; Gavrilov, AV; Eropolov, VA.*J Mod Opt*, 2007, 54, 833-844.
[13] Carpenter, J; Thomsen, BC; Wilkinson, TD. *J Lightw Technol*, 2012, 30, 3946–3952.
[14] Koonen, AMJ; Chen, H; Boom, HPA; Raz, O. *IEEE Photon Technol Lett*, 2012, 24, 1961-1964.
[15] Carpenter, J; Wilkinson, TD. *J Lightw Technol*, 2012, 30, 1978–1984.
[16] Hoyningen-Huene, J; Ryf, R; Winzer, P. *Opt Expr*, 2013, 21, 18097-18110.
[17] Chen, W; Wang, W; Yang, J. *Opt Expr*, 2013, 21, 25115-25119.
[18] Tsekrekos, CP; Syvridis, D. *J Lightw Technol*, 2014, 32, 2461-2467.
[19] Svistunov, DV. *Techn Phys Lett*, 2004, 30, 332-334.
[20] Svistunov, DV. *J Opt A Pure Appl Opt*, 2004, 6, 859-861.
[21] Svistunov, DV. *J Opt Technol*, 2012, 79, 29-35.
[22] Asawa, CK. *J Lightw Technol*, 2002, 20, 10-18.
[23] Unger, HG. *Planar Optical Waveguides and Fibers*, Clarendon Press; Oxford, 1977.
[24] Olshansky, R; Keck, DB. *Appl Opt*, 1976, 15, 483-491.

INDEX

J

L

M

N

O

P

Q

R

S

T

U

V

W

X

Y